THE SPY

By the same author

The Learning (1988)
McElhinney (1989)
Northside (1990)

THE
SPY'S WIFE

◆

A TRUE ACCOUNT OF
MARRIAGE TO A KGB
MASTER SPY

Janet Coggin

CONSTABLE · LONDON

First published in Great Britain 1999
by Constable and Company Limited
3 The Lanchesters, 162 Fulham Palace Road
London W6 9ER
Copyright © Janet Coggin 1999
ISBN 0094 79490 1
The right of Janet Coggin to be identified as author of this work
has been asserted by her in accordance with
the Copyright, Designs and Patents Act 1988
Set in Monotype Garamond 12½pt
by Servis Filmsetting Ltd, Manchester
Printed in Great Britain by
St Edmundsbury Press Ltd
Bury St Edmunds, Suffolk

A CIP catalogue record for this book
is available from the British Library

To the memory of
MAURICE COGGIN

ACKNOWLEDGEMENT

Thanks to Jeffrey Simmons

Preface

It is, I have always believed, the writer's job to impart truth; not to present a clever conclusion, not to reveal some great universal secret of life, not to dare to presume to teach, but to convey, if he can, a glimpse of that recognisable truth which links men and women to each other and to the world, even to those who have lived before and those yet to come. It is not for the writer to strive to convince, but to appeal to the already existing insight of the reader, to his capacity for understanding the mystery of existence, with all its beauty, sorrows, ugliness, joys and fears; all its intricacies.

To write with the aim of conveying truth of any kind, the writer must search within himself, and in that 'lonely region' he finds the impressions and observations that have become one with him during the course of his life.

The Mahatma Gandhi called his autobiography, *The Story of My Experiments with Truth*, and this is surely what all our lives are about. Like gold-panners we sift and sluice away the illusions and delusions, the lies and falsehoods, until only pieces of true value remain.

In one sense every life is different, in another every life is the same; the circumstances may be unfamiliar, not the feelings and emotions they evoke.

This book about Lilian Hentze is the story of a large part of my own life. Everything in it happened. It is a story, not of espionage but rather, one could say, of the effect of one person's espionage on another – or, more correctly, on many. I have presented here facts, and shown how they affected me personally, (I speak for myself only), and the repercussions which follow me to this day; without casting aspersion on the character of others, believing as I do in each person's privacy and the right to be themselves. However, having said that, I must assert also the right to be myself; to feel free to think about, write about, look at and examine what after all is my life – after so many years of being obliged to be reticent, evasive and secretive to those most close to me, for fear of harming or implicating them.

I suppose it was when I realised that I had spent most of my years of motherhood being grateful for not being murdered, and of course at the same time hoping that I wouldn't be, that I decided to explore just what had brought me to this preposterous state of affairs.

Part One

———◆———

I

When Lilian Hentze (whose true name is altered for the duration of the book) heard with incredulous ears the familiar voice of her husband, whom she had always understood to be simply a naval officer, telling her that he was in fact a Russian spy, a master spy he would have her believe, who ran a spy ring in Europe – and had been since even before they were married more than eight years ago – her immediate reaction was one of relief and hope. Did that mean he was not mad? That there were perfectly normal explanations for his insane behaviour?

In her mind she saw herself taking some laundered sheets to the walk-in airing cupboard, with a mind to arranging them on the shelves; she saw herself opening the door, felt the shock as Carl, six foot three, burst out from the dark interior, shouting furiously at her.

She could, of course, have demanded an explanation, but her instinct advised against it, for indeed what reasonable explanation could there be? Was she prepared to hear Carl say something like, 'Sorry to startle you, Lili, but I thought I was a bear and I was looking for somewhere to hibernate.'? No, she definitely was not, for then there could be no more evading the issue; serious steps would have to be taken, unpleasant facts faced – the worst of which being the possibility that her children (the joy of her life) could be inheritors of madness. So she had said nothing, just put the sheets away and closed the door, closing also the door of fear in her mind.

There had been too many, an accumulation of, like incidents, such as when he had asked her for a box of matches which he had left on a table and later was not there. She had offered to fetch some more from the kitchen and he had banged his fist down on the table and roared that he didn't want other matches, he wanted the box he had left on the table. Or the time she had gone to retrieve a child's toy, left in his study, and walked quietly behind him as he sat working. He had jumped up with a raised arm and said through his teeth, 'Don't ever do that again, or I might kill you!'

Now she asked for explanations and he, amused rather than contrite at the recollections, told her that he had been developing a microfilm in the airing cupboard; that he had written a code number in the matchbox, and that he was trained to kill, in three seconds flat, anyone who came up silently behind him. It was important, he said, that she realise what a strain he lived under.

They were walking as they talked. She had been surprised when he had suggested an evening stroll, it was unlike him, but now he was explaining that he couldn't talk of these matters in the house; the house, he said, was bugged. Yes, he said, it always had been – it was a fact, something one simply got used to.

He appeared to be enjoying himself and his expression had taken on a cunning aspect. Suddenly all Lilian's hope and optimism started to fade; he's madder even than I thought! A complete lunatic! Delusions of grandeur!

'I don't believe you,' she said wretchedly, 'you're fantasising!' She looked away, focusing her eyes on the African scenery, which until now had always given her pleasure.

As if from a distance she heard him say, 'No, I'm not. I'll show you something when we get back to the house, I'll give you proof. But just don't talk about it while you look; keep on talking about something else, the children or anything you like. It's not difficult to get the habit, once you are aware of the problem.'

Still not knowing whether to believe anything at all that he said, she had flared, 'I find all this disgusting. Did it ever occur to you I might not want to live in a house that is bugged? Is this your rotten sense of humour . . .? Or, if it's true, why didn't you tell me before?'

'Ah!'

'What do you mean, ah?'

She saw from his face that something more was coming. But what? Hadn't he already surpassed all limits?

It was now conveyed to her that 'they' (the Russians) wanted her also to work for them. She was being recruited! Was it possible!

It was necessary, he told her, that they, he and she, become a husband-and-wife team.

'Necessary for whom? For the Russians? For you? Or for me and the children?'

It wouldn't involve much, he said. Just travelling around Europe from time to time, as a courier. It was convenient she had family in Europe (her mother had been Danish), it would allay suspicion – and she liked travelling, didn't she?

Believing, and yet still not believing, she stopped walking and stared at him. 'Lots of people enjoy travelling, but I wouldn't imagine they all want to be couriers for the Russians! And how do the children fit into these plans of yours?'

He continued to walk and she had to follow, 'It needn't affect them.'

'And if you are caught?'

'I won't be.'

'Too smart, eh?'

'That's right.'

This is a ridiculous conversation, she thought. It's unreal! And I'm not even touching on the real issues; the morality or immorality of it all; at any rate what I believe about lies and betrayal, cheating and deception. And I should ask him his reasons. After all, to betray your country, your friends, your profession, you must need a pretty powerful motive. Was it for his ideology? – He had never seemed to have any. Or for money? Surely to God they had enough as it was. Power? Or perhaps some sort of inner hatred, wanting to get his own back on someone or something? Or had he simply been lured by illusions of glamour and excitement, seen himself as a James Bond figure? If what he'd said was true, he had been practically embryonic, when they got their clutches on him. Yes, he had been the 'best Cadet' of his year; won the Queen's sword as a prize, she had presented it in person. But it would be useless to ask him for reasons, he never said the same thing twice; he would give you a different answer every time. She had long got used to it. If anyone asked her what he thought about apartheid, or politics or religion – or anything, even his favourite music or sport, she would reply, 'Ask him yourself, I haven't the faintest idea!'

Once, in earlier days, she had questioned him as to why he did this to everyone, and he had replied carelessly that he liked keeping people confused.

They walked on in silence, then Lilian said, 'Well, you can count me out! I hope you realise that.'

'As you like, no one's going to force you. But think about it, take your time before making your final decision.' He said this in a conversational tone, then turned and gave her a hard look. 'But if you decide not to do as you are requested, I'll have to find someone who will. See what I mean? It's required that from now on I operate as a husband-and-wife team.'

'Suit yourself!' Lilian replied in a quavering voice.

When they got back to the house the children were asleep and the housekeeper was in the kitchen. Carl took Lilian into his study and showed her a letter. 'What do you think of this?'

It was typewritten and from someone in England she had never heard of. It went something to the effect of, 'Dear Carl, It's some time since I last had news of you, so I thought I would drop you a line. How are Lilian and the children? Hope to see you next time you are over in the UK, Yours, Denis.'

While she read, he talked blandly about some book he pretended to have been reading. 'What do you think of it?' he repeated.

'Pretty boring,' she said. The coldness of her voice was directed at him. How could he talk normally, as if nothing unusual had happened? It was inhuman beyond belief.

'Nondescript, wouldn't you say?'

'I would.'

'Well, do you think this is an improvement?' He indicated a minuscule black spot on the notepaper, so small she hadn't noticed its existence, and handed her a high-powered magnifying glass – something she had never seen the like of.

She peered through it and saw that the dot consisted of a whole block of writing.

'Oh God!' she mouthed, and sat down weakly. She desired only to go to bed, to lose herself in sleep and to wake up the next morning as if nothing had happened; but it was out of the question now, she had left one world behind and entered another; a world that seemed to mock all she had ever believed in; a world of deceit where even she was now tainted, for she would never again be free to be completely open with family and friends, for fear of implicating them; a world that threatened her children.

Her sense of outrage was all the worse for its impotence; Carl, after all, had chosen for himself, she and the children had not. Against their will and without prior knowledge, they had been spewed, like so much rubbish, into an abyss that had no light, no firm ground, where anything could happen.

During the next days, the talks that followed proved something on the scale of a nightmare; Lilian insisted she wanted nothing to do with any form of espionage, that she only desired to bring up her children in peace and safety. He said he understood and would help her leave, but again, she did realise, didn't she, that he would have to find someone else, preferably already on the Russians' payroll; and as for safety, she must know that wherever she went there were people who could find her and question her. Methods of questioning, he said, varied. It was known for plastic bags to be put over heads of children, and the mother forced to watch their faces turn purple – to encourage her to talk.

Other veiled threats and warnings followed; it was the beginning of the realisation that she must be very careful. Wanting now only to take the children and leave, she accepted the things he said in a matter-of-fact way, as if they were discussing or conversing the way normal people did, and as if she had no personal views or opinions what-soever.

She did, of course, but they would have to wait. There would be time for that later — she knew she would have to work out her own feelings, her own position; how she felt about things. Simply by the fact of what he had told her was she now an accomplice? A traitor? By not informing on her own husband, the father of her chil-dren, did that mean she condoned what he did? Nonsense of course, but what about legally? Or again, to hell with legally, what about morally? And then, she had never believed in divorce. Hadn't she promised 'For better, for worse . . .' and all that? And really meant it? But, too, wasn't responsibility to her children the overriding reason for her whole existence? All these questions would have to be gone into in detail before she could feel intact again, but not now. The only thing to think about now was action.

Boat tickets were purchased, a removal firm sum-moned. Packing up was painful, but a resolutely cheerful front was maintained for the children who, fortunately, were accustomed to the naval pattern of moving house and travelling. The day for leaving came; both parents cried at the parting, they were not yet thirty.

Lilian's childhood and youth had passed more or less uneventfully; her memories were almost entirely of riding around the countryside of Devonshire, first on a small moorland pony, later on a beautiful thoroughbred horse, for the most part content and at one with the world and nature. Her home had been simple and unostentatious, her family consisting only of her father, an older sister and a nanny, at least for the early years. There had been friends, too, with whom she liked to go boating, and she played tennis from time to time in green gardens, the players sitting around afterwards on lawns, eating raspberries and cream.

When she had finished college and most of her friends had gone up to London to share flats and find jobs, she had worked in refugee camps, for it was the time of the 1956 Hungarian uprising in Budapest, and she had been moved by the photographs in the newspapers of distraught families arriving in Britain. While thus employed, by the United Nations' Aid to Refugees programme, she had returned to Devon for an old school friend's wedding (the marriage was to a Canadian naval officer) and there met Carl. Within a few months of only meeting now and then – when either his or her circumstances permitted – they had become engaged, and shortly after married. Her only recollection of that period was that he had somehow eclipsed both her work and the rest of her social life. Nothing else had seemed to matter. She was twenty-one then, and a year later they had their first child.

Like all naval wives, she learned to pack up house at short notice and set off with her growing family for unknown destinations, wherever her husband might be posted. And when the fleet he was attached to would leave again, she would watch the long line of grey battleships steam from whichever bay or port it happened to be, then repack and return to the UK to wait for further instructions.

When they were together there were always social events, balls and dinners and cocktail parties, which inevitably palled after a while, but there were exciting things to do, too, new opportunities, new sports to try out, like (and this for her was a revelation) learning to fly the little Tiger Moth planes. Skimming low over the fields, then flying upwards until you were looking down from a height, looking down at the world through only a pair of flying goggles seemed the most glorious new pastime. Following rivers from their source down to the open sea and then soaring out over the watery expanse of the channel, glimpsing the boats below, with their foamy wakes trailing out behind them, was surely the nearest thing to the freedom of being a bird – and with an instructor in the seat behind, who would take back control if anything got difficult, it was entirely pleasurable and easy, like practically everything else in her life.

She grew to be adaptable, to enjoy the movement and variety of a naval existence; she liked moving from place to place, renting houses, living one moment in Malta, their balcony overlooking the blue Mediterranean sea, and the next to find herself shovelling snow in the garden of a charming old cottage in Kent. It was all in the luck of the draw, for there could be dreary places, too, dreary beyond belief, but not for long and these you could put down to experience – it was interesting, after all, to know how other people lived. Not that such questions touched her as deeply as they might. For her, she was simply Carl's wife, the mother of their children, and she had no wish to change anything in her life.

Nevertheless the changes came, the first being the big move to Capetown. Carl had been born in South Africa at the time when it was still a British possession. On joining the navy he had been given a basic training there and then sent to England to specialise in engineering, at Manadon Royal Naval Engineering College in Plymouth, and it was during this time that he had met Lilian. When South Africa and England parted company, as an officer in the Royal Navy he had been in the position of being able to choose which country he wished to serve, and naturally enough had chosen the land of his birth. So it was that after some years of both training and service, the time had come to return.

Lilian had no qualms about the move; she knew they would be back regularly for Carl to do further courses in the UK – and the lure of Africa was great. Thinking only of the scenery and wildlife she and the children would see, the exotic fruits they would taste, the heat and the colour (and never having had a television or been particularly interested in reading newspapers), she was totally ignorant of the political and social aspect of the country; had never heard of the word apartheid. The sum of her knowledge of life, so limited, came only from what she had seen around her as she grew up. The school she had attended, if not exactly a seat of learning, had been, in its own way, quite genuinely a place of education, at least in certain aspects, for it was made up of pupils, boys and girls, from all walks of life and all parts of the world – colours and physiognomies varying accordingly. This fact in one respect saved her, for she was never able to accept the barrages of brainwashing she was subjected to in her new country of residence. But in another respect it caused her untold loneliness, for it presented an insurmountable barrier between her and those white South African acquaintances she was expected to become friends with.

Her father had tried to warn her before she left England.

'You are in for a horrible shock,' he told her. 'You ought at least to be prepared.'

He had been uneasy, to say the least, about her marriage to Carl, and she had put it down to quite natural fatherly feelings.

'Nonsense,' she had protested mildly, with that enviable surety and logic of the young. 'There's good and bad everywhere, it won't be any different in South Africa.'

The decks of the ship (it was one of the renowned Castle Line) were packed to capacity. Lilian and Carl, crammed with all the other passengers against the rail, leaned over the side, looking down to where, far below, the narrow strip of black oily water between the massive hull and the quay was gradually widening.

Lilian had said her goodbyes down in Devonshire, and now she tried not to think about it, to feel instead a pioneering spirit, and to be caught up in the excitement of the moment. A band was playing the sort of rousing marches designed to instil courage, or lend cheer to festive occasions. Thousands of coloured paper streamers, flung continuously into the air, were cascading down the side of the ship, down to the tiny swarming figures on the dockside who appeared to be running around, trying to catch them; something to be occupied with during the last and hardest moments of parting. Like others around her, Lilian's face was running with tears. She remembered her father's expression and how Carl had said, 'Don't worry, sir. I'll take care of her.'

She turned to him now, 'I'll go down to the children. I don't like leaving them in the nursery with strangers.'

She had collected them, and taken them to the roomy cabin that was to be theirs for the voyage; and they had comforted her, as only small children can. Later, when the crowds had dispersed somewhat, and she felt it safe to take them on deck, they had gone to find Carl, and together, cheerfully now, they had stood at the rail, holding their children in their arms, watching England recede, become a long thin line on the horizon and then finally vanish.

For two weeks there was nothing to be seen but sea and sky, sun, moon and stars, dolphins, whales, flying fish and clamouring seagulls. At the beginning of the voyage they had wondered how they would fill the timeless void that stretched out ahead of them. After a few days they never wanted it to end. How sordid it would be to have to go again in noisy cars and trains; to be obliged to think about timetables and shopping, all the responsibilities of life. What more could one want than this? What greater peace and tranquillity than to lean over the stern rail and watch the wake spreading out behind the ship, like the tail of a comet endlessly changing colour; the white foam becoming immersed in shades of red and gold during the long sunsets, silver under the moon.

The navy had paid the passage of course – first class – and the sumptuousness of the cabins, dining room, ballroom, lounge and other rooms took no time at all to get used to. Why not, after all, have an orchestra, discreetly half-hidden behind potted palm trees, to play to you while you eat, and be served exquisite food from silver dishes? Why not dance in a subtly lit ballroom to a good dance band, before drifting out to watch the stars reflecting their light into the ocean?

After they had passed through the Bay of Biscay the days grew hotter, the nights languid. Passengers sat on deck talking, reading or just staring at the sea and the sky, exerting themselves only to move their deck chairs further into the shade. Stewards appeared at intervals with cool drinks and refreshments, occasionally bearing news that dolphins could be seen sporting themselves on the port or starboard side of the ship, or flying fish, or whales; this would be the big event of the day, everyone trooping over to the rails to watch.

Days, blue and dazzling, drifted one into the other. The ship pressed on, almost sullenly now, towards the equator.

The heat was becoming oppressive, deck sports such as quoits and table tennis ceased; the swimming pool was deserted, the water in it, once cool and refreshing, seeming to seethe in the hot sun.

Two days before crossing the line, stewards carried tables out onto the shaded deck and covered them with white starched tablecloths. The number of passengers who still had appetites had reduced dramatically; many now just lay all day in their cabins, sweating into their sheets, lacking the energy to move further afield than to their bathrooms. Lilian and Carl, probably the youngest of the first class contingent – which tended to be made up of rather elderly couples and apparently successful business-men – were fortunate in that none of their capacities were so seriously impaired that they could not enjoy or do justice to the outdoor meals – an enticing array of salads, cold cuts of meat, fish, lobster and other shellfish – while sipping small quantities of chilled white wine and looking out from their shade at the brilliance of the sky and water around them.

Children, on the Castle Line boats, were catered for separately; meals specially prepared to suit young tastes were laid on one hour before the adults ate. Mothers and fathers sat with their children, helping them to choose from the menu, and afterwards accompanied them to the airy nursery where they would be read to and cared for while the parents attended to their own needs.

The outdoor dining arrangements lasted for four days in all, before normality (now that the line of the equator was falling away behind them, temperatures mercifully dropping) reigned once more. The hush of fatigue that had fallen upon the ship lifted; the sounds of table tennis and quoits could be heard again, splashings in the swimming pool, restrained laughter and animation.

Carl and Lilian had become used to the decks being almost empty, now suddenly there seemed to be people everywhere. They joked among themselves: 'The oldies are all appearing again, like beetles coming out of the woodwork.'

'I had forgotten half these faces, hadn't you?'

'No, I just thought they'd all crawled away to die.'

In the evenings the band played as before, dancing was resumed. Most nights now the young couple were joined at their table by a man, slightly older than themselves, whom they had come to know on the trip. He told them his name was Robert McDaid, that he was divorced just recently, and little else; obviously he was depressed and glad of their company. Until they had invited him to join them, that is for the first part of the voyage, he had sat alone at a small table, dark and morose, probably bored in his isolation (later he explained he had been annoyed at being obliged to wear evening attire – everyone dressed for dinner in the first class).

Despite his rather long reticent silences, he seemed quite at ease with the two of them, although when he did talk it was about nothing in particular, nothing you would recall afterwards, certainly nothing you would connect with him. Years later Lilian remembered only his appearance; the narrow moustache, the white teeth, the dark heavy eyebrows, even the pale hands with long fingers, but nothing of his essential character. She imagined this might be due to his domestic troubles and pitied him, he gave the impression of a kind and decent person, but somehow lost.

Now and then he would ask her up to dance; he was a good dancer and she didn't believe him when, out on the floor, he smiled and said, 'I don't really like dancing, you know. I only do this to give your poor husband a rest!'

In the daytime Lilian's favourite place was the children's nursery, probably the pleasantest room on the boat. Here she would join in the play with the various toys, or sit in a comfortable chair and read a book while her children made their own games of imagination, hearing from time to time their shouts of laughter and excitement. Sometimes she would stop reading and just watch their glossy heads, bent over, engrossed in whatever they were doing.

Little by little, shipboard life assumed the illusion of reality; this was the real world here, everything that was taking place on land seemed unreal, insignificant, much ado about nothing. And the small cosmos, with its accompanying cloud of seagulls feeding daily from the galley scraps, moved on almost imperceptibly, for the scenery was always the same.

Finally, however, even the fact of not wanting the voyage to end was powerless to detract from the magic of that pearly morning when, at around 6 a.m., the ship steamed silently across the glass-still water of Table Bay and Lilian looked up for the first time at the great flat-topped mountain.

2

The bedroom curtain, white muslin, moved slightly. A bee was caught in it; it buzzed at intervals and appeared to get itself further bound up in the folds. Heat simmered outside in the garden, the scent of summer flowers hung undispersed in the still air; and from half-closed shutters, bright light fell in strips across the dark wooden furniture, the polished floor, the white cotton bedspread on which Lilian lay, debating whether or not she had the energy to get up and free the captive bee.

Only recently returned from the military hospital, where her appendix had been removed, she still took, when she could, the opportunity to rest, usually while the children were at playschool or having their after-lunch nap. Carl was at sea, his ship not due back for several weeks, and she was glad of it. She couldn't imagine how other married couples got on without breaks. People would say to her, affectedly she thought, 'Oh my dear, how do you manage with a husband who goes off to sea, and leaves you to cope alone?'

For her the space was essential, without periods to herself she felt she would be lost. Yes, it was better that he should be at sea now, she felt relieved of his presence which of late had become something of an accusation. She needed time to think; so many things were hard to accept, to digest, to comprehend or come to terms with in her new life and she had been shocked to find a lack of communication growing between them, widening into what could become an abyss. Hesitant of appearing too critical, too disapproving of what was after all the society of people he had been reared amongst, she needed nevertheless to express her surprise, distaste even, at certain attitudes in her new environment.

But somehow it hadn't helped to talk about it with Carl, he hadn't wanted to discuss, only rather to tell her, and she was aware of his annoyance that she was neither willing nor able to be guided by him. He wanted, he said (and she felt it more an order) to see her fitting into her surroundings, being happy, so that he would have no worries and could thus get on with his work unhindered. She had everything, hadn't she? She should consider herself lucky.

When they had first arrived in South Africa, and moved straight into naval married quarters, Lilian had felt quite pleasantly overwhelmed by the friendliness of the families she met. Carl was evidently a popular figure among the other young officers and their wives, and had been missed during the years of service overseas, particularly by the group he had done his initial training with. Clearly glad to have him back, they all made a point of welcoming her, too, with great kindness, reassuring her that she would feel at home in no time. The women presented her with cakes and biscuits they had baked especially for her – she would be too busy, they said, settling in these first weeks, to think of baking – and invited her to their houses for coffee mornings while Carl would be at work, and of course to bring her children so that they could make friends with their own.

As a couple they were invited for dinners in many homes, both English-speaking and Afrikaans. Carl pointed out that this was unusual, to say the least, as the two were not inclined to mix. He, however, had a foot in both camps, for his parents, Germans, had immigrated before his birth, and he spoke German, Afrikaans and English, each as if it were his mother tongue.

Certainly she soon noticed for herself that the Afrikaaners, (descendants of the early Dutch, German and French settlers), seemed to dislike the English quite intensely, mostly for historical reasons but also because they were convinced the English looked down on them in that way the English have rather a reputation for. Whether or not this was so, it was true that, at least within naval circles, there was practically no fraternisation between the English and Afrikaans families.

She used to wonder why, when among Afrikaaners, people kept coming up to her and saying things like, 'Ah,

Carl's Danish wife, welcome!' Or, 'Let me introduce you to Carl's Danish wife!'

'Why have you told everyone I'm Danish?' she asked Carl, for he had never remarked on the fact before, in all their married life. 'You know I've never lived there.'

'Your mother was Danish.'

'That never interested you before. Why *suddenly* am I Danish?'

'Only when we are with Afrikaaners; it makes you more acceptable to them. You can be as English as you like with the English families.'

'I don't "like" to be anything, and I don't enjoy having to "be acceptable" . . .' She saw there was no point in continuing, Carl had a characteristic way of storing details, and using them to his advantage when he saw fit, and this business of her being Danish was clearly useful to him.

For the first few weeks, Lilian found herself woken several times each night by the tramping boots of armed guards, passing close by the house.

'Why on earth . . .?' she asked Carl from where she stood at the window, looking at the receding figures and their guns, having leaped from the bed the first time she heard the noise. Outside the harshly lit street and houses looked more like a prison camp than a collection of family homes.

'People here,' he told her, 'mostly the women, are a bit neurotic – haven't you noticed yet? You will. They don't feel safe unless they are surrounded by guards and guns . . .

they've all got guns in their cupboards; whistles hanging around their necks even! They'll start telling you soon. I wouldn't take much notice, if I were you – they create their own fear.'

He was right. They did start telling her. And giving her advice.

'Look,' said Carl when she repeated it to him, 'listen to them if you have to, to be polite, but don't take it in.'

So she didn't. It sounded sick, as if they had discussed their dreads and fantasies so often, they had finally turned them into reality, at least for themselves, to the point they felt obliged to make their lives around safety plans. One woman, whose husband was going away for two months, told Lilian she had brought her son back from boarding school to 'protect' her, and had a new, more solid front door fitted. Others, when their husbands were at sea, went home to visit their parents or had friends to stay, anything not to be left alone.

'Why are they scared?' Lilian asked Carl. 'Everything seems so quiet and peaceful.'

'Guilt,' he said, looking amused – she never knew what he really thought about anything. 'They are afraid of getting their come-uppance. And you have to know that things are only quiet and peaceful because of an iron-fisted control system; if it falters, God help us all! But it won't, at least not for a good many years.'

Uneasily she felt the weight of her ignorance. She remembered her father's warning, her own self-assured reply.

She took to listening carefully, paying full attention to everything she heard said or implied; watching how people behaved, attempting to understand what was going on around her. She felt as if, with the shake of a kaleidoscope, everything had changed utterly and she suspected that instead of the beauty she had anticipated, somewhere a terrible ugliness lurked.

She continued to go to coffee mornings and tea parties, on her own or with the children, and to dinners with Carl; but was aware of a slow sense of withdrawal. She realised it finally and fully while listening to a conversation at a coffee morning on the subject of nannies. One young woman, with a pinched face and rather long teeth, was bewailing the fact that her children's nanny, the most 'kind, honest, reliable, thoroughly decent' African woman (who incidentally had been her own nanny when she was a child, and then her sister's, and therefore had been with the one family for twenty-six years) was leaving. And did anyone know of a good nanny available whom she could employ in her place?

'Why is your own nanny leaving?' asked Lilian, moved by the story of some twenty-six years of dedicated service.

'Ah,' responded the toothy woman, smiling as if she had some wisdom to reveal, 'she started to have troubles. And take my word for it, my dear, when these people start to have troubles, it's time to get rid of them.'

'What do you mean, troubles?'

'Oh, the usual sort of thing. She started by saying her mother was in hospital, and could she have the day off to visit her. And could she borrow some money for the train fare to wherever it was, Bloemfontein or somewhere. Then she wanted to go every week, said her mother was dying – well, I mean, that could take months! After that there was some story about her nephew, I can't remember what it was now; and then there was something else, something about her brother, sick or in prison or something . . . I could see it was going to be endless, so I told her the time had come for us to part. She was terribly upset, poor thing, but I had to be firm. That kind of thing goes on for ever, once it starts – there's no end!'

'It's true,' another young mother affirmed, noting Lilian's unconvinced face. 'Take it from us, we've lived here all our lives, we know how things are.'

'Don't look so worried!' The plump, overdressed hostess of the morning chided her, laughingly. 'We'll all help you, and guide you until you find your feet.'

She had been thankful when both she and Carl had seemed to think of moving house simultaneously. She imagined their needs to be the same, to get away from the closed-in atmosphere, the over-familiarity of the naval circle and find somewhere where as a family they could enjoy freedom and the beautiful Cape scenery. For him there could have been more on his mind, a need to have isolated surroundings in order to carry out his network of communication, but of course she wasn't to know or guess at this. The blame for their desertion was laid on her shoulders – the naval quarters weren't good enough for

her; she thought herself above them all. Carl, much enter-
tained, repeated the gossip to her, and while she ignored it
as untrue, it never occurred to her that he might himself
have manoeuvred these rumours in the first place, and
then enjoyed their circulation.

The house they found, in Noordhoek, on the west side of
the Cape Peninsula, was set some way back from a six-mile
long beach, with pristine white sand and large soft waves
rolling continuously in from the Atlantic; and not another
house in sight. Inside it was cool and airy, every room
having french windows leading out to green lawns, trees
and flower beds. Over to one side of the garden, by some
pines, was a swimming pool – not of the garish blue
kidney-shaped variety – but a proper one, with a convenient changing hut for guests, who tended to come
unasked on Sundays, bringing droves of offspring,
nannies, friends, dogs or whatever; the house unfortunately being just the right distance into the country for a
Sunday outing, which included a breath-taking scenic drive
on the way.

Further afield was a large and productive vegetable
garden, hedged by tall trees and wire-fenced to keep out
baboons and deer. At the rear there were stables and out-
houses. A gardener went with the house, practically a
condition of sale, for he lived nearby with his large family
and was anxious not to lose his job when the property
changed hands.

For Lilian, the best part of the house was the stoep; a

shady terrace looking out to sea; bamboo-roofed, bougainvillea covering one wall, a vine making its way up the other. Here she could sit and read, or watch the children playing in the garden from a comfortable old wicker chair. Here she felt she could while away the years in content, watching her children grow to maturity – she had no great ambitions for them; simply that they would be decent and kind people, and that they would find their paths in life, whatever was right for each one of them personally. She found it hard to understand the importance attached to power, success, status – empty things so far as she was concerned. She had been working in a refugee camp when she had first come to know Carl, and had been relieved to meet a young man without ambition (as he had declared himself) who simply did his work because he liked it. He had seemed so sane compared to others she knew, already clambering and jostling to get a foothold on the ladder of success. She wasn't to know it was a simple technique of his to listen to a person's views and then, when they had forgotten the conversation, voice those same sentiments as his own. And at the time she had been delighted; felt they were both free of the harness that most young people seemed to find it necessary to strap themselves into.

Of course by now she had realised he was indeed ambitious, almost immoderately so, she thought, starting sentences with, 'When so and so goes . . .' as if senior officers were ninepins, to be bowled over on his way up, obstacles in his plan of progress; or 'When I'm an admiral . . .'

'You really shouldn't wish the years away,' she said to him, 'Why do you think you'll be happier when you are a fusty old admiral? These are probably our best years now!'

And he was successful; assiduous hard work brought rapid promotions, ever more gold braid – how much of all this being a smoke screen to cover other activities, or how much that he was simply an achiever in whatever he did, or how much that he genuinely cherished the career he had chosen as a lad, cannot be surmised. Perhaps he didn't know himself; sadly, it is in our youth that we need wisdom, for it is then we do our sowing; by the time we reap it is too late to change the seeds we sowed.

And Lilian, too, was mistaken. Despite all that portended well, those years did not turn out to be their best; not for either of them, and for entirely different reasons; reasons which took their separate tolls.

Just as guilt can cause unhappiness, so equally unhappiness can cause guilt; that is to say, if we live in a utopia and are not happy, we are inclined to feel guilty about it. Thus when Carl had told her accusingly, that she had everything, and should consider herself lucky, she had felt almost a criminal. She had so much, much more than most people; as well as having lively healthy children, she had the loveliest house she had ever seen, unbelievably beautiful surroundings, no money or health worries, people working for her – Teena in the house, Harry in the garden – and didn't she even have her own horse to ride across the six miles of white strand below the house, and a pony for the children?

Recently English friends had visited and, standing out in the garden, surveying their home, had said, (not trying to conceal their good-natured envy), 'You two don't know you're alive! This is unreal, a dream!'

Why then did she feel an intangible darkness closing around her, something heavy and thick, threatening, obstructing? Was it that she felt herself in the presence of some evil? Was she struggling against it? Or against the desire to give in to it? It would be so pleasant not to acknowledge that her ease, the ease of all whites in South Africa, had been wrought and sustained at the cost of profound anguish and excessive toil of the natural-born owners of this land.

'No man is an island, entire unto himself.' And more's the pity, Lilian thought. Beginning to feel the less she had to do with other people, the better, she would vastly have preferred not to budge from her small world of Noordhoek at all. Everyday life, however, being what it is, she was obliged to go shopping or take the children to kindergarten in the nearby town of Fishhoek, or drive to the naval dockyard in Simonstown – all of which meant passing by a large Coloured settlement most days of the week. 'Coloureds' or 'Cape Coloureds' as they were called, (people of mixed blood or from other non-European parts of the world) lived here in a mean, straggling encampment; their homes corrugated iron shacks, their cooking facilities fires outside their doors. On windfree days, as you approached, you could smell the woodsmoke and feel cooking-grime in the air from a good way off. Here naked or half-clad children played games, or ran or crawled on the baked mud between the shacks; some sitting along the roadside, watching the cars go by, laughing and waving trustingly, slapping at flies, brushing them from their hot bodies.

She never learned to pass without cringing; just as she never learned not to cringe as she watched black nannies, in their brightly coloured uniforms, walking with their small white-skinned charges along the beaches, in front of the 'Whites Only' notices – black skins only permitted providing they escorted white children, never their own.

She came to feel that every time she went out there was some kind of unpleasant incident that spoiled her day. She never forgot the very first time she went shopping. Carl had dropped her off in Simonstown and said he would be back in a couple of hours, he'd pick her up at the central square. Simonstown in those days was like a tiny Wild West one-horse town, with rickety wooden-fronted shops with posts and railings outside; you half expected a posse to gallop up and throw the reins of their horses over the rails.

She had finished her shopping and then gone to the square to wait. Finding an empty bench in the shade she had sat down thankfully, for the day was hot and, being early, she had some time to pass. Having many things on her mind she was not sure how long she sat there, but after a while she had noticed some tired looking Africans, elderly, with parcels, standing nearby and wondered why they didn't also avail themselves of the long wooden bench. She moved herself to the far end to make more room for them and their parcels; they watched her, nodded even and exchanged polite smiles, but continued to stand, wilting in the heat, occasionally moving from one leg to the other.

When she saw Carl and walked over to him, he greeted her with, 'Good God, Lili, what were you doing sitting on a bench for non-whites? Couldn't you have looked at the notices and found one for whites? There's twice as many. Those poor people couldn't sit down, you know, once you were on their bench. You must learn,' he added, 'that *Blankes Alleen* means Whites Only, and *Slegs vir Blankes* strictly for Whites.'

She hadn't wanted a servant; she had made it quite clear from the start; she didn't like the word 'servant', she didn't want anybody calling her 'madam' and she certainly didn't want anyone wearing a ridiculous undignified uniform on her account.

'You had house help in England,' Carl pointed out.

'Yes, and I was glad of it. It's the one time in your life you need help, when you have young children. Years ago there were grandmothers to help, and aunts – now everybody is doing their own thing.'

'Well then, why not have house help here?'

'In England I felt it was a job like any other. You are not a servant – you are filling someone else's need, and being paid a proper wage for it. I wouldn't mind doing it myself, if the other person had young children and I hadn't.'

'You've just got a hang-up about the word servant,' Carl

[43]

said. 'It's inverted snobbery! Why not have house help here, as you did in England? Pay the same wage as you did in England, if it makes you feel better – and forget the word servant.'

'It could be, you know,' he added, 'that you think a little too much about yourself, what's right for you personally; not enough observance of what's going on around you, the status quo; people here need work, they need it badly, it could make all the difference to one person's life to work for us.'

Silenced and uneasy, in the face of what he'd just said, she could think of no reasonable argument.

The next day Carl arrived back from Simonstown with an African woman sitting in the back seat of the car. He got out and she followed him, pulling an old suitcase after her, and came to stand beside Lilian, shading her eyes from the sun with one hand, smiling broadly with unconcealed pleasure.

'This is Teena,' Carl said, 'she would like to work for us.' He turned to the woman, 'Isn't that right?'

The woman nodded, cast her eyes down shyly and a small gurgling laugh escaped from her mobile mouth. 'Yes, madam,' she said.

She seemed to be wearing several garments, shabby but good colours and somehow stylish the way she had them wrapped around her. She was tall, unhealthily thin. Her head, turbaned with a bright cloth, was almost skull-like, with sunken hollows in the cheeks, but she held herself proudly erect and her eyes were honest and good.

'Oh, and she would like to live in,' Carl added, as if he had forgotten to mention it. 'She hasn't anywhere else.'

The woman nodded again and pointed to the case. Her smile increased. 'Nowhere to go, madam.'

Lilian felt she was making her last stand. 'Teena,' she said, 'do you think you could manage not to call me "madam"? I mean you can call me Lilian, or Mrs Hentze, or anything else you like – or even not call me by name at all, but please not "madam".'

'Yes, madam! Whatever madam likes!'

She lost out over the uniform, too. After a few days, Carl passed on to Lilian the information that Teena was feeling embarrassed, inferior, beside the other nannies, her friends, who all had their uniforms bought for them.

'But we can give her money to buy whatever clothes she likes. She has got a great eye for colour and style.'

'She wants to be the same as the others. Can't you see it from her point of view?'

'I suppose I must try,' Lilian said, abashed, wondering how on earth she would get to terms with seeing this vibrant, clever-looking woman wearing flunky's apparel and calling her madam. 'But why does she tell you, and not me? I would have thought, being a woman . . .'

'She knows you are from overseas, that you don't understand things here.'

Teena's home was in the Transkei, a poor area designated for the Bantu people – a Bantustan – in the eastern part of

Cape Province. All the able-bodied men and women of the Transkei were obliged by the poverty of their land to leave their children with the grandparents and come south for employment, sending their wages home to keep the young and elderly from starvation. Sometimes Teena would return home for visits. The first time she had re-appeared carrying a baby on her back. It was forbidden for black Africans working in white suburbs to have their children with them, but now, living in Noordhoek, a country area, with no one around to see – having her own bedroom and bathroom in the house – legal or not, no objection was made by Carl, and Lilian was delighted. In the mornings while she and Teena did the housework, two babies now occupied the playpen instead of one.

The result of Teena's second trip had been a little girl of about ten years.

'Who's this?' Lilian had asked.

'Elsie, madam,' was the explanation. 'Elsie my niece. Elsie look after babies.'

So Elsie did, and there was more fun among the children than ever.

Later there was a suitor too, a pleasant and intelligent man who worked in the Forestry Department up in the mountains whom she married in due course. He used to come for weekends whenever he could take time off from his work.

It had seemed a good time then. When Carl was at sea and there was no socialising to be done, Lilian would do one big shopping session with the car, stock up the house

[46]

with food and whatever was necessary, and then simply not budge off the premises, unless for some unavoidable reason. At night she would sleep with her windows open, the curtains only half drawn, so as to wake to the calling of wood pigeons in the trees and the early morning sunshine filling the dark corners of the bedroom.

These were periods of great peace and harmony as far as she was concerned, as long as she didn't think too deeply. She enjoyed doing the daily chores with Teena; she rode her big white horse on the beach; she swam; she painted in oils; above all she saw her children, and Teena's, happy. She enjoyed Harry's presence around the place, too; he, always so amiable, so good with the children, and she was glad knowing that his work provided his own family (he had seven children), as well as hers, with all the vegetables they could need.

Yes, things were good . . . and yet they weren't, and she knew it. She saw Teena content, she saw Harry content (or so it seemed, but how could you know?); she felt content herself, but the knowledge was there that her utopia, instead of having blue skies, was enveloped in a cloud of pollution because in the end, no matter what one thought or did, or what was in one's heart – simply to be white and living in the country was an insult to its people, a form of condoning the laws of inequality and discrimination, injustice of every kind.

One night, or rather early morning, around 3 a.m., the phone beside the bed rang and without switching on the light she reached for the receiver, glancing at the same time at the luminous hands of the clock. The ship must have docked in Simonstown, she thought. It'll be Carl wanting me to pick him up. Unusual though, at this hour.

It was not Carl's voice. An operator told her there was a call coming through from Johannesburg, and then an unfamiliar male voice said, 'Hello! Carl?'

'Carl's not here,' she said. 'It's Lilian. Who is that?'

'Ah,' the voice sounded hesitant, reluctant even. 'Robert McDaid here. Do you remember me? We met on the boat – Southampton to Capetown. How are you, Lilian?'

'Fine, thank you, and of course I remember you. It's good to hear you.'

'Carl's away then, is he? When do you expect him back?'

'In about a couple of weeks, I don't know the exact day – he's at sea.' And then she couldn't refrain from adding, 'But . . . well I mean, isn't this an odd time to call?'

'Ah,' again the moody reluctance. Then a sigh, together with the grudging admission, 'I was feeling depressed. I get lonely sometimes, can't sleep. It's the divorce – still getting me down.'

'You mean you ring Carl . . . for a chat . . . when you feel depressed?' It was almost unthinkable – she couldn't imagine Carl in that role.

'. . . I can't bear to think of Ann with someone else!'

'I'm so sorry,' she said wretchedly, inadequately, 'I really am. It must be unbearable. Look, do you ever come down this way? To the Cape? Do come and stay, have a bit of a break, a change. It might help.'

[48]

He mumbled some kind of thanks then and rang off, rather abruptly. She lay in the dark feeling sorry for him, trying to recall something, anything, about him but details were strangely lacking. She couldn't even remember what he did for a living, what his work was, and certainly not what his interests were. Then her thoughts turned to Carl; for the life of her she couldn't see him as confidant or counsellor, discussing matters of the heart with a friend. But she was glad; it was after all a side of him that she herself had not discovered.

And she did not think twice when, in the future, her husband would get up at unusual hours and say he would take a call on another phone, in his study, so as not to keep her awake.

3

It was time to visit Carl's mother. The original plan was that she should come down from Pretoria where she lived, and stay with them in the Cape for some weeks or even months; but lately she had been having health problems and did not want to be away from her doctor. Carl was only due ten days leave just then, but it was decided that a quick trip up to Pretoria would be better than nothing. The longer visit could still take place as soon as she felt more able for it. Naturally she was longing to see her sailor son again, and to become acquainted with his wife; also of course she wanted to see her grandchildren.

They drove up through the green fertile valleys of the Cape, paradise of the first settlers, where crops grew high, cattle grazed luxuriantly and vines in neat rows encompassed gabled homesteads, shining white in the sun. Further on, the scenery changed to the flat semi-desert vegetation of the Great Karoo, empty and treeless. Carl told them they would not believe it was the same place if they came through in the spring, for the bare ground would be covered in wild flowers, just for a brief period after the rains. The highway on which heat danced and wavered stretched straight ahead without bend or curve for as far as forty miles in some places. At intervals, rusting carcasses of wrecked cars had been hoisted up onto posts at the side of the road, as a warning to drivers not to lose concentration or sleep at the wheel.

It was a relief eventually to notice a gradual change as little by little the landscape grew softer and became grass-covered. Finally it gave way to rolling African veldtland, scattered with sheep, stunted acacias and dwarf mimosas, the horizon broken at times by long mountain ranges. Now and then hot, dusty little villages appeared and vanished, each much the same as the last; a main street lined with parched jacaranda trees, small mean houses with trellised verandas, dry gardens where scrawny hens scratched among the roots of hibiscus and kumquats.

They stopped in one such village, or dorp as Carl called it, to buy soft drinks from a general store. Lilian followed Carl up dilapidated wooden steps onto a broad stoep, where ferns grew in rusty tins and bored mongrel dogs scratched their fleas and watched newcomers with dull eyes. Soiled netting hung across the doorway in an unsuccessful attempt to keep out insects. Inside, unpleasant smells of rancid cheese and other decaying foodstuffs hung thick in the air; flies crawled on strips of dried raw meat, biltong, which was strung from the rafters; and unkempt children, some white, others black or in between, stood or crouched – big eyes staring from behind open sacks of unsifted meal, dried beans, rice, sugar and flour. On the counter, brightly coloured sweets stuck, melting and sticky, to the insides of dirty glass jars with hand-written labels: Sugarsticks, Niggerballs.

At the counter sat an old man with heavy flabby skin and rheumy eyes that were shrewd nevertheless. Carl bought cigarettes and Coca Cola for himself, lemonade for Lilian. The drinks were lukewarm. They drank them quickly, gave back the bottles and returned, bloated and unrefreshed, to the car where the children slept fitfully, shaded by sheets hung over the windows.

'What an awful place,' Lilian said, trying to imagine the daily existence lived out by the inhabitants of these small, half-dead dorps, miles from anywhere.

Carl did not seem affected one way or another. 'It's a poor area,' he said, 'but they could do more with it. It's their own fault.'

'But in such a rich country? Can't people be helped?'

'Not these,' he said. 'Not Poor Whites.'

'What do you mean "Poor Whites"? You speak as if they were a separate race, not just white people who happen to be poor.'

'They don't just happen to be poor, any more than other people just happen to be rich. I'm telling you, no white person needs to be poor in this country, not if he is pre-pared to work. But the Poor Whites – and they are in fact like a race apart, inbred and hopeless – they don't want to work, they don't want to learn. They are what you might call the dregs, the rejects, substandard; looked down on by everyone, even by the kaffirs.'

Was there any end to discrimination in this country? 'That man,' Lilian asked, 'that man in the shop then, was he what you'd call a Poor White?'

'Yes, but he's better off than most. Characters like him make quite a little fortune for themselves by swindling the kaffirs. You might be surprised at how much he's got put away in a tin somewhere.'

'And the children?'

'Probably all his. Contravention of the Morality Act is rife in country areas.'

'You mean the law forbidding sex between white and coloured races? That people get imprisoned for? How can they consider it a contravention of morality? It's people's own business. Anyway, how can they enforce it?'

'Well naturally the police are not going to waste their time coming to dorps way out in the bundu like this, in the hope of catching some lecherous old devil fornicating in a ditch with a munt.'

Sometimes she believed he spoke like that on purpose – to punish her for her views. They drove on in silence.

It had not been difficult, on arrival in Pretoria, to feel comfortable and at ease with her mother-in-law. The German woman had given her a warm and enthusiastic welcome and wept tears of happiness over her son and grandchildren. For Lilian, whose own mother had left

home and babies to drive ambulances in Poland at the out-
break of Hitler's aggressions, and then chosen not to
return, it was pleasant to feel she was acquiring a motherly
sort of friend, someone with whom she could have
leisurely discussions about family and domestic matters.
And despite the attractions of Pretoria city, with its fine
buildings and beautiful parks, on the whole, while Carl was
out visiting old haunts and acquaintances, she preferred to
pass her time with Mrs Hentze in the cool house that smelt
of flowers and wood and polish, watching the children
play in the garden, and talking over the joys and difficulties
of childcare, for there was not in those days the vast array
of books on the subject that can be found in bookshops
today.

And here it was that she first got an inkling of her
husband's childhood; how he had suffered from his
father's violence and his mother's unhappiness. When she
learned that at the age of thirteen he had scraped tablets
from his mother's mouth to prevent suicide, she felt she
could hardly bear to hear more.

With each day, Carl seemed increasingly ill at ease in what
had been the home of his childhood. Too many bad memories. So when he told his mother he wanted to take Lilian
and the children up country to show them the Kruger
National Park, spend a few days going through it, Lilian
made no objection. Even though her heart ached for the
older woman, it seemed better not to show she noticed the
slight. Her mother-in-law appeared, at least on the surface,

delighted with the idea: 'Of course! What a wonderful experience it would be for them!'

She still could not manage to pronounce the English W, and the combination of her enthusiasm and the word 'vonderful' was touching somehow in the face of what must have been her disappointment.

However, Carl's transparent relief as they set off on their expedition was reason enough for Lilian to be glad, too, for the recent revelations of what he had been through in his early life had shocked her, and she pitied him deeply. It was the first time in her life she had heard of marital violence and abuse to that extent (hard to imagine in these days of television and gossip magazines) and she pictured her absent, divorced father-in-law as a mixture between Frankenstein and a sort of Dr Jekyll and Mr Hyde, rather than what he probably was – a totally mixed-up and mentally unstable person, who might have had other sides to his character as well. When she tried to imagine this man, and the terrible things he had done, and then compared him with her own father and the secure childhood he had given her; how there had been hardly a cloud in her sky, riding her pony through the woods and fields and valleys in Devon – she felt she was only just starting to open her eyes to the outside world.

Anyway, she thought, why could not they, herself and Carl, together make some good come out of it all, phoenix-like; wasn't that the way – to cancel bad with good? For wasn't there all the more reason for Carl to want to give his own children happiness and security? To want harmony in his family life? What, after all, could be a better way of closing the door on his past?

After the Mediterranean-type climate of the Cape, the further north you go, the more intensely you feel the magic that is Africa. At least that was Lilian's impression. All during the drive from Pretoria to the Kruger Park, the colours, mainly ochres and siennas, seemed to cry out at her from the rocks, the high sere grass, the dried-up river beds, and of course the brilliant blue sky.

Although for the most part there were no people about, life nevertheless teemed everywhere, all around, but so quietly, blending so naturally into the landscape, you had to look to see it – be ready for unexpected appearances, as some creature, an impala perhaps, would break cover, leap and then vanish. Or a snake wriggle across the road into the undergrowth. All the time there was the contrast of sudden movement and then silence. From time to time great herds of wildebeeste could be seen grazing in the distance, and birds of all sizes flew from tree to tree.

Once they stopped at a crossroads to let a group of Africans pass in front of the car. They were all – both men and women – so tall, so black (almost blue-black), so stately and regal in their bearing it would be unthinkable to drive by, sending road dust flying up at them. Some were carrying things on their heads. The others inclined their faces politely, indifferently, and they all moved on towards a river that had water in it. A boatman was waiting.

'How can they wear those heavy woollen blankets

wrapped round them?' Lilian whispered, in a kind of awe that almost forbade speech. 'They are beautiful colours, but it must be so hot.'

'The opposite,' Carl said. 'That's how they keep cool. They probably think you are mad in your thin things.'

She hadn't known Carl was carrying a gun, but at the entrance lodge of the Kruger Park he produced it, as was apparently customary, and had it wired up by an official. This meant you could still fire it in the case of emergency, but you would have to show it on leaving, and be called upon to give an explanation. Investigations would then be made to verify the situation.

The Park, the largest game reserve or wildlife sanctuary in existence, was a world in its own right. Once inside, you were asked to obey certain rules. One was that you should on no account get out of your car or stroll from it, and another was that by 5 p.m. everyone should be inside one of the many enclosed camps, and be accounted for. Maps were handed out so that visitors could calculate at what point, and at what time, to head for the nearest campsite.

So they explored, taking this road and then that, which-ever attracted their fancy. And everywhere indigenous animals, such as previously seen by Lilian and the children only in zoos, now graceful and dignified in their natural state, grazed and foraged, stretching out necks to find favourite leaves or tender shoots, so completely in their element that the odd passing car did not even cause them to turn and stare.

The camps – all the same – were encircled by high walls, and consisted of round brick huts with thatched roofs, rondavels; one for each family, or person if travelling alone, and there was a large communal restaurant. At five in the afternoon the gates were shut and later, lying in bed at night, elephants could be heard trumpeting, or lions roaring, and there were strange snufflings that seemed to come from right outside the window, a whole cacophany of unfamiliar and faintly unnerving sounds.

By the third day they felt they must have seen every kind of animal that inhabited the Park, except elephants. Which was strange. Although their droppings were plainly in evidence, huge mounds, freshly steaming sometimes, for some reason it had been impossible to catch sight of even one. And Carl, who by now seemed to think he had made the journey solely for the purpose of viewing elephants, was growing increasingly annoyed.

'It doesn't matter,' Lilian said, several times, 'if we don't see them this time. There will no doubt be other occasions. And you've seen them before. So let's not spoil the day!'

But by now he had become single-minded. Driving angrily back and forth over the network of narrow roads, disregarding the twenty-five mile an hour signs, sometimes going as fast as sixty, he refused to be diverted by conversation, and was clearly unmoved by the fact that the children now sat silent and uncomfortable, no longer enjoying the expedition.

Mystified, Lilian recalled another time, their first holiday together, before any of the children were born;

they had gone to ski for two weeks in Austria, and when they arrived there was no snow. And until the snow had come, several days later, Carl had been so furious he had been unable to accompany her for walks in the mountains, or around the village, or even to try out the restaurants. He had simply lain fuming on the bed, reading whatever books (dog-eared old thrillers) the hotel could provide. It was somehow as though he hadn't the ability to deal with, or cope with, situations that were beyond his control.

He refused when she suggested they return to Pretoria now, earlier than planned, pointing out they still had two days left, sentencing them to two more days of flying grimly round the Park at sixty miles an hour, everything depending on whether or not an elephant could be spotted. She attempted, but it was of no avail, to tell him to snap out of it – he literally could not.

However, the next day they were mercifully saved from the ordeal by freak weather. Shortly after they set out to hunt elephants, there was the most almighty crash of thunder which, going by the blue sky above, was so unlikely that at first they thought it must be something else, although no one could imagine what. Then it happened again and within minutes the sky had become grey and closed over, the temperature fell to freezing, and hail-stones the size of hen's eggs were dropping haphazardly onto the car and all around.

They had only just passed a small game lodge, so Carl turned the car round, made the distance back and pulled off the road under some trees. Then, covering their heads, he got them all into the lodge. Within a few more minutes the hailstones were falling thick and fast. Another man joined them in the lodge but he left his Mercedes out in the road, unprotected, and when the hailstorm abated and they went out into the sunshine, his car had been dented and crumpled almost beyond belief by the hailstones.

Later in the day the real storm came – the hail had been merely the hors d'oeuvre. And this time they were miles from a lodge or any of the camps, so they were obliged to press on regardless through the bursts of torrential rain, the thunder and lightning, their headlights on for the sky was dark now, trying to stay on the tarmac, which was eroding fast.

Once they saw two green lights shining towards them, and as they came nearer they realized these were eyes, and were able to make out a magnificent leopard standing at the side of the road.

After that, they half drove and half slid down a hill, only to discover at the bottom that a river – newly created by the storm – now crossed their path and they could go no further forward. And while they were surveying the swiftly flowing water, considering the possibility of fording it, just driving through and hoping for the best, a thump behind them, followed by another, announced that two trees had fallen and the way back was also blocked.

'I'll go and inspect the water,' Carl said, opening his door. 'See how deep it is.'

'We're not supposed to leave the car,' Lilian said nervously. 'There are leopards and all sorts of things out there.'

'Don't worry, I've got the gun. You stay put with the children, and whatever you do, don't open any doors or windows.'

When he had gone she tried not to imagine him being torn apart by the leopard, and chatted instead with the children, who obligingly thought it an exciting adventure. There was no real danger as long as they stayed in the car. Even if they had to wait until the next day, someone would come and rescue them. Carl, however, could not stay in the car. He would come back, report on the state of things – the depth of the water, the rocks which had fallen – and then vanish into the darkness again.

In fact they were rescued that night. When it was reported they had not turned up in any of the camps by 5 p.m. or left the Park, a patrol was sent out to look for them. For the children, half-asleep, it was the highlight of the trip, being towed through the river by Land Rovers of the Game Reserve rescue team.

4

Behind the swimming pool there was a piece of scrubland, still their property, that dropped gently down the hillside towards the beach. Through it ran a path and at the bottom was a wooden fence and a gate. It was the way down to the sea, and Lilian loved this bit of land because it was wild, no one had ever attempted to cultivate it; flowers in their original state grew among the scrubby bushes, straight out of the dry earth – gladioli, irises, lilies, delicately coloured, infinitely more beautiful than the forced varieties we have become accustomed to. If you walked this way it was necessary to wear boots, especially in the hot season, because snakes lived here, but mostly Lilian would pass through on horseback, sometimes leading the pony with one or more children on its back.

She was surprised one weekend when Carl told her to put boots on and come down to the scrubland, and the more so to find empty tin cans perched on each post of the wooden fence.

Handing her a small revolver, a Browning .22, he said, 'I think the time has come.'

'Time for what?'

'I want to teach you how to use it.'

'Who says I want to use it? I thought you were against all this neurosis about guns!' (How could he just U-turn like that!)

'Well, try and see it my way. When I'm at sea, I get to thinking about you and the kids alone here. I want to know that if anything happened, you could handle it.'

'If what happened? Why all this suddenly?'

'It's OK.' He spoke as if calming her down. 'Everything's OK at the moment. But the situation may deteriorate in the future, and I want to be sure you and the children are safe, as far as possible. Look, nothing is going to happen. Think of it as a bit of target practice – for fun! Come on, you know you'll be good at it!'

'Well,' Lilian said, tempted, 'all right then. I've always been quite a good shot at funfairs.'

He showed her how to load and reload; how to fix the safety catch; and they spent the rest of the morning shooting holes through the tin cans. She was nowhere up to his standard, but not bad just the same and, forgetting entirely the grisly reasons behind the game, gave herself up to enjoying the competition.

'Leave the cans where they are,' he said when they had finished and were walking up the slope towards the house.

'You should practise at least once a week, more if possible. Every day if you can.'

'Ah no,' she said, 'It was fun today but . . .'

'I'm not talking about fun now,' he interrupted. 'I want you to do what I tell you. And you're to keep that gun, loaded, in the cupboard in the dressing room – on the top shelf, so the kids don't find it.'

Still walking beside him, she ceased to listen to his words. She saw the long beautiful house with french windows, the green lawns; Teena laying lunch on the stoep; she saw the hibiscus flowers, the jasmine and bougainvillea, and heard the children's laughter as they chatted with Harry in the vegetable garden, pulling their small pony behind them on a rope.

Carl was still talking: '. . . and from now on I want you to put it in the glove compartment of your car, whenever you leave the house.'

It was neither Lilian's nature, nor her style, to have rows. When she felt strongly about something, she would take her time, think long, and then try to communicate her feelings through exactly the right words, so that the other person could be left in no doubt whatsoever as to her opinions or views.

'I'll think about it.'

'Do me a favour,' he said. 'Don't think, just do it!'

Just do it, he had said. Don't think, just do it! Didn't he understand she had a mind of her own? Didn't he know that a decision on whether or not to carry a loaded gun was fundamental to who you were? You didn't just 'do what you were told'; you thought it through and what you finally decided was who you were as a person – that was your self.

He was going to sea again next week, probably for about a month. That would give her some time to think the whole question over. It wasn't just a matter of her own personal ethics this time, she had the safety of the children to think of, it was her responsibility to make the right choice. In the meantime, she knew she would be unable to prevent him from putting the gun on the top shelf of the cupboard. His mind was set on it, and that evening he gave her further instructions on what to do in the case of emergency.

'If you should hear them out in the garden one night,' he said, (unspecific as to who 'them' meant – Coloureds from the nearby settlement? Or Africans from further afield?). 'If things sound suspicious and you think they are going to break in, get the gun quickly and pull one of the heavy armchairs over to a corner of the room – a corner with no door or window, of course – then get the children and yourself behind it and wait. Whatever you do, don't fire as they come in at the doors or windows, hold your fire and wait. Wait until they come up close, then put them down one by one. It's just a matter of keeping calm and concentrating on one at a time.'

That night she had a nightmare; something rare for her, normally she only had bad dreams if she had a fever. She saw that it was night and the garden full of human shapes, black faces hidden among the trees, moving here and there; sounds and then long silences, then sounds again. She led the children up the steps into the attic, and after bolting down the trap-door, huddled together with them in fear. Clattering footsteps from below, within the house, told her that the marauders had broken in. 'They won't find us,' she kept telling her children, making her voice sound confident. Then she smelled smoke, heard crackling sounds, and realised the house had been set on fire. Now she must choose whether they should be burned alive, or go down and in all probability be hacked to death by the enemy. She was still frantically trying to make up her mind which to do when, mercifully, the dream came to an end, leaving her trembling and sweating in the peaceful dark night.

It took a little time to understand fully that the nightmare had been purely the result of inculcated fear, nothing else, no other reason at all, and of course in turn it generated still further fear in Lilian. After Carl left to go to sea, she had a telephone extension put beside the bed. She would do rounds of all the doors and french windows every night; locking them, later checking she had done it properly, and then anxiously re-checking again just before she went to bed. In the daytime though, dark thoughts evaporated in the bright clear sunshine; then it was as if nothing could attenuate or distort the joy of seeing her children, happy, free and healthy, playing in what surely was the nearest thing to Eden – an oasis of green lawns, wood pigeons calling in the trees, coloured butterflies hovering among scented flowers and tall grasses; the backdrop of timeless white sands and rolling blue coaster waves.

One particularly hot noon, too scorchingly hot even to be on the shaded stoep, Lilian, helping the children to re-arrange their rooms, hang pictures on the walls, left them to go in search of some nails and a hammer. The garage at the back of the house was large, built to take several cars – and deep, fitted out as a workshop at the far end. Coming as she did from the shimmering, almost white heat of the day and the racketing of uninhibited cicadas into the sudden dark silence of the garage, was like walking into total blackness.

Feeling her way past the cars to the workbench at the rear, she groped about, running her hands over various tools on the bench, and then, hearing a sound, looked sharply right to where it came from. In what was now a dusky half-light, she saw the whites of a pair of eyes, white teeth, fully exposed. She could not see the dark face clearly but recognised Harry's smile. Her glance took in a metallic glint and she saw instantly that his hands were sharpening the broad blade of a large, vicious-looking panga. Still smiling, he picked it up and looked at it, weighing it in one hand, running a finger along its side.

So this was it! She was never to forget that moment of pure animal fear, and how her thoughts went to her children, waiting for her.

With eyes now re-adjusted to the dimness of the garage, she looked into his face and saw infinite kindness in his smile. It was as though he both understood and lamented her terror.

'Madam is looking for something?'

Forcing normality, she said, 'I came for a hammer and some nails. I'm putting pictures up for the children.'

That incident, small as it was, proved to be a turning point, a milestone; furious with herself and deeply ashamed of her fleeting suspicion, she saw with perfect clarity that fear had been engendered in her (where previously none had existed) on no evidence whatsoever. In future I shall go only by what I see, she thought, and what I feel. Something tells me that Teena and Harry are probably the most decent people I have come to know in this country; I will listen to that voice, and trust my own judgement. If it turns out to be wrong, I shall be obliged to blame myself; better at least than having to blame myself for trusting to someone else's judgement.

She was appalled now by the memory of her target practice with Carl, the morning spent firing at the tin cans – what, after all, had they been doing, but practising how to shoot at black people? It was obscene. And Teena, hanging out their washing, would have seen them at it; Harry, too, passing by as he tended their garden; both would have been fully aware of the implications – and they themselves not permitted to own guns. It had been a display (even if unintended) of power and control. Her shame was unbounded; it was she who was making herself their enemy, not the other way around. And then, on top of that, she herself this day had nursed suspicions of Harry. It was total madness.

Before he left Carl had spoken, sensibly enough it

seemed at the time, about the children and about her responsibility for their safety. But to her the issue seemed so much wider than taking a gun wherever you go. First of all there was the responsibility of setting an example, doing the right thing, being the right sort of person. After that one had to think about what must surely be the effect on children of having fearful parents – for the one (the gun) presupposes the other. Almost certainly it would be to make them fearful, prejudiced people themselves, unable to live happy, healthy lives, unable to make unclouded judgement on anything. Finally there was the question – does living with a loaded gun actually ensure children's safety? She hadn't in fact read in the newspapers of families attacked in their homes, but she had read countless reports of fatal accidents, children finding loaded guns in drawers and cupboards of their homes.

Just as one makes a decision whether to trust or not to trust, so, in most cases – not all – one makes a choice whether or not to live in fear. At this point Lilian decided that she would trust her own inner voice, and that she would not live in fear. She ceased her paranoia about the doors and widows, gave up locking them altogether, and took the gun and buried it in a far corner of the garden, down beyond the snakes and the scrubland.

During that period she continued to believe (she wanted to believe it, she needed to, in fact she had never even contemplated the possibility of not believing it) that the best times, the happiest, were when they were all together as a family. Years later, in retrospect, she knew this had not been the case. As a couple they had aspired to harmony, but not achieved it. They had done things that were generally considered as 'having a good time', and people would remark on them as being an 'ideal family' – unfortunately it was not so.

From the early days of settling into their new life in the Cape, they had travelled, making expeditions of the longer kind when possible, but more often nearer to home, taking advantage of days of leave, here and there, between Carl's sea appointments.

At first Lilian had enjoyed these trips, setting off early before the sun got hot, then getting out of the car and walking in the valleys and mountain foothills; picking wild flowers and bringing them back to learn the names, Afrikaans names; slangboom, bakkiesblom, rooipijpie, sambrieltje, for the country in itself was very close to paradise, dangerously so – it could make you forget everything else. But always these outings would have some sort of a bitter ending, and she would finally become depressed. Why? She couldn't put her finger on it at first – Carl's irritabilities, mood swings over trivialities, or so it seemed.

Sometimes they would go down to Cape Point, the end tip of the peninsula where the coastal scenery was quite exceptionally spectacular – gigantic cliffs and rocks jutting up from white foam, sunlight glittering on dark sea. From the road you could see herds of wildebeeste grazing among long grass, and baboons strolling and quarrelling,

like gangs of delinquent children. They would climb on
your car if you stopped, and try to stick their fingers
through the windows. Carl would be laughing; they would
all be enjoying themselves. Then suddenly, for what
seemed like no reason at all, he would become furious
about something, something someone said in all innocence, or goodness knows what.

Naturally it had an inhibiting effect; both Lilian and the
children felt the constraint of having to pause and think
before everything they said or did. The children would
become frightened and silent, and Lilian, unable to con-
ceive of why a minor annoyance such as, for example, an
insect finding its way into his coffee, could bring about so
great a display of frustration, even fury, and such questions as whose fault it was, would wish they hadn't come,
were back at home just getting on with normal everyday
life.

5

The black woman let herself in at the kitchen door and, stooping, lowered her suitcase and some parcels wrapped in brown paper onto the floor. The baby on her back started to cry and the girl, Elsie, took him off to their small apartment. The woman continued to stand by the doorway, head bowed, shoulders hunched. Lilian, washing salad at the sink, looked up. 'Teena! It's your weekend off, I thought you'd left at the crack of dawn as usual!' Then, looking more carefully as the face was raised towards her, a face bruised, swollen, hardly recognisable, she cried, 'Good God, Teena, what happened?'

Turning away to hide her humiliation, Teena related her story; she had gone to visit a cousin in one of the locations outside Capetown, but just beyond the train station, practically on entering the location, she had been beaten up and robbed of her wages. Unable to face her cousin, and no money now for the train, she had walked back under the hot sun, her baby on her back, Elsie at her side helping with the suitcase and parcels.

'Why didn't you ring me? You could have reversed the charge – but you didn't know, did you? Come on, we'll go into the drawing room while I ring the doctor. Don't bring that kitchen chair – come and lie down on the sofa.'

But she brought the kitchen chair – what madness it all was. The doctor's number was written up by the telephone. 'Yes, yes, of course I'll come over at once, Mrs Hentze,' he said. 'Somebody attacked and beaten up did you say? Ach, that's terrible indeed! A friend of yours, is it – a guest staying in your household?'

Needless questions! Why didn't he just come! 'She lives here. She's my maid.'

'Your *maid*!' An irate voice now, 'You mean a *Bantu* woman? Or *Coloured*!'

'He flatly refused to come,' Lilian told Carl when he came home from the dockyard, starched white uniform, gold epaulettes, a different world from the one she had just been faced with. 'He all but said he wasn't a *vet*! It was unbelievable; and there was Teena, barely conscious, still in shock, sitting stiffly on a kitchen chair because she couldn't bring herself to use our comfortable armchairs or sofa!

'In the end we went to some squalid clinic for Non-Europeans, a nightmare, overcrowded, nowhere to sit, and waited for hours. I could see what an ordeal it was for her – and she would probably have been better off at home, lying on her bed – but we both felt she should be checked over first, after a head-beating like that. Thank God there is no permanent damage, but it will take her some time to recover, and to get over the shock too, emotionally I mean.'

'You mean to say you rang Doctor Kramer to come for Teena!' Carl said, scandalised amusement, which seemed to border almost on satisfaction, moving across his face. 'Good! He's always boasting about his liberal views. This might force him to look at himself!'

Was he concerned about Teena's misfortunes, or more interested in the doctor's political hypocricies? The truth was, she simply did not know this man she had chosen to spend her life with; she had no idea still, after five married years, of what was important to him and what was not. The fact that he could hold a certain opinion one day, maintain the opposite the next, and again something totally different at any other given moment, left her floundering as if the ground were continuously shifting beneath her feet.

At the same time, trying to be fair, she could see that he, too, perhaps even more so, was having problems with her. How must he feel, after all, to find he had brought to South Africa a wife who baulked, who criticised, who barely managed friendly acquaintanceship with the other naval wives; who kept a disapproving distance from the very people and way of life he had grown up with? It couldn't be easy for him, or pleasant. Perhaps he wished now that he had not married in England, but waited for his return

to Capetown and then found a born and bred South
African girl who would suit the life, enjoy it and be a help
in his career. With sincere remorse Lilian would attempt
reparation in spasmodic bursts, but without real success,
for one cannot change oneself for the sake of expediency
– although she sometimes had the feeling that this was
what he expected of her. She said to him once, in a
moment of dispassionate curiosity: 'Which would you
prefer, for me to be a sort of puppet-wife, who does and
says and thinks what you want her to, or a real human
being who thinks and acts according to her character, her
nature?'

With a smile which by now she could read as: You think
I'm joking, but I'm not, he had replied, 'A puppet-wife, of
course!'

Around this time neighbours, white women, in groups of
two or three, started to pay her visits. They were concerned about her treatment of Teena. 'You're spoiling her,'
they said, 'paying too high wages, giving her your
unwanted clothes instead of selling them to her, as we do
to our servants. She won't appreciate you if you make
things too easy for her.'

'Actually, it's her who makes things easy for me.'

But they overruled her. 'Take our advice; we *know*, my
dear, we've lived here all our lives. We are just trying to help
you.'

'Yes,' came the back-up, 'that's right! So you can avoid
making mistakes.'

[75]

Later the gist of their conversation shifted somewhat, their voices adopting a stronger tone: Their maidservants, they told her, were friends of Teena's; knowing her conditions they were becoming dissatisfied with their own, and it was making them lazy and sloppy in their work – rude sometimes even. It was quite intolerable.

'Don't listen to them,' Carl said, when she told him. 'Don't let them intimidate you.'

'But why are they like this? It's so hard to understand. They all, whites I mean, seem normal enough people in most respects; they love their children, and husbands or wives or whatever; they are good to their friends, even to their animals – but when it's a question of a person with black skin they seem to lose all sense of humanity. There's no respect, no opportunities, no justice for black people in what is, after all, their own country!'

'You just have to grow up, that's the real problem,' Carl said, irritation rising. He spoke slowly and deliberately, as if to someone of reduced intelligence: 'Can't you see it's impossible to treat people as slaves if at the same time you regard them as equals? It wouldn't be Christian, would it? And white South Africans are very Christian – haven't you noticed them all going to church on Sundays? Look, Lilian, try to understand that these people cherish their way of life, which is sustainable only through the labour, the exploitation if you prefer the word, of the blacks. So what can they do? They invent learned and eminent professors to prove that indigenous Africans are not fully human, rather more akin to apes – and that makes it OK to use them as slaves, for all the work they don't want to do themselves. However, not being as totally dishonest as that view requires a person to be, some doubt remains, the consequence of which is guilt – and guilt, as we all know, generates fear and hatred.' He paused and his face seemed to glare at her. 'Do you understand now? Got it? Good!' He appeared disgusted with the subject, and her: why couldn't she leave things alone? Why must she interfere? Why couldn't she be like other people? There was nothing she could do about the situation, so why not lie back and enjoy it – like everyone else did?

She didn't particularly like the way he said it, his manner, but she had to admit it was probably a reasonably accurate picture he had painted of the social scene, and, after all, he was right in a way – effectively it was like that, whether she liked it or not, and it was true, too, that there was nothing she could do about it. Therefore it was up to her to decide on her own personal position. His view was that she could either put up with it, accept it, try to enjoy it even – or simply shut up and not be criticising everybody. What other alternatives were there? She could leave the country, of course, refuse to be a part of the injustice and exploitation, but she wasn't in fact prepared to break her marriage, to split the family over it. In that case, it seemed that the only path left open to her was to continue to concentrate on their own small cosmos, and here again she had to admit that Carl, despite his protean attitudes and moods, was never anything less than fair and decent in his dealings with Harry and Teena, and that their conditions of work were as they would be anywhere in Europe, possibly better. The fact that on the larger scale, in the world beyond these narrow boundaries, they, and all black people, would go on endlessly being subjected to every kind of indignity, their children never offered the opportunities that Lilian and Carl took for granted for their own, was something already settled, which Lilian had to accept she had no power to alter, or even influence. That was the way it was.

'All right,' she said to Carl, after thinking for several days about what he had said. 'I will do my best in the circumstances, and I won't complain and criticise – but don't ask me to take the one step further of pretending to like people whom I despise for their inhumanity, their cruelty, their selfishness.'

'Don't be so rigid,' he told her. 'It's just that they don't think.'

'You're probably right, and if I were a better person myself I could perhaps like them genuinely, forgiving them on the grounds that "they know not what they do", but I haven't reached that stage yet, and pretending is something I can't do. And I can't while away time with them, listening over cups of coffee to their complaints about their servants, their preferences concerning hairdressers, or their gossip about whoever doesn't happen to be in the room. Don't ask me to.'

They considered it a truce of sorts, but for Lilian it remained a time of isolation, of uncomfortable and disconsolate thoughts: if she cared enough would she break her marriage and leave? On the other hand was she rigid? Unbending? Did 'growing up' mean relinquishing values – swapping them for different ones, according to what country you lived in, or which society you were trying to become a part of? To please other people? For expediency? She had not been reared to any doctrines, but had simply grown up believing that the way to behave was with common decency to everyone, that it was a universal value.

If it was difficult for her, only a few years out of the cocoon, so to speak, it must have been equally so for Carl, with the difference that he had been raised with the South African outlook, and now was having to ask himself what impact his educators and countrymen had made upon him, and what he actually thought himself. Sometimes Lilian tried to imagine herself in that position; born in South Africa, growing up watching her parents, teachers, friends' families, the way children do . . . in those circumstances what might she have come to believe, think, feel? It was a sobering thought.

She missed the sane company of her father, and of past friendships and, when the loneliness became too acute, she would ride her horse down on the long sandy beach; wade him through the shoaling water to cool his legs, and fix her eyes far out to sea, as if some answer were to be found there, drawn from the blue horizon where all appeared clear and serene. Here she did not feel so alone; here it seemed she could escape the insistent thoughts, the compelling preoccupations of self, and join company with an impersonal longing, as of all mankind longing for the impossible.

They were talking about her, Carl said, around Simonstown, in the naval circles. It had started with the wives, but now even the officers in the mess were making remarks. He didn't look as if he minded too much, and she was relieved. 'What are they saying?' she asked.

'That you don't go to the wives' coffee mornings any more.'

Had he forgotten their conversation, their truce? 'Well,' she said, 'it's true, as you know.'

'They say it's because you are stuck up, think yourself superior. Naturally I tell them it's not that at all – it's just that you are a difficult sort of person.'

'Oh, thanks!'

'Well you are, you know. You can't deny it. You've got all these ideas of your own which you brought along with you – which are not applicable here – and you just can't let go of them. You hang on at all costs, like a dog with a bone.'

'Look, I've been doing my best to keep my opinions to myself. But because people know I have them, they are determined to convert me; they see it as their mission. They won't leave me even to think my own thoughts in private.'

'Why mind? Why not simply go along to be friendly? You English are supposed to be so diplomatic! Why not make the effort just to please them, just to oil the wagon wheels? And,' he added, 'you don't have to look like a dying duck. What's wrong with you?'

Disheartened by a sudden longing to be accepted and liked, she was thinking: yes, what *is* wrong with me? Maybe it *is* my fault, maybe I'm not handling things the right way. 'I don't know,' she replied drearily, and was shocked to hear her voice sounding tearful, 'I really don't know.'

He was quick. 'Perhaps you should see a psychologist? I could arrange it for you. There are some good ones in the navy.'

'A psychologist!'

'Don't look like that. I'm only trying to help you.'

'Everyone's trying to help me.' She turned her head aside to hide her face.

'There's no hurry,' he told her. 'We'll get you some vitamins first, or iron tablets. You could be run down – you do look a bit anaemic, come to think of it. We can talk about a psychologist later. Meanwhile I'll make a few enquiries. I heard there is a good man in Simonstown – Joubert, I think his name is.'

'There is nothing wrong with me,' she said. 'I don't need your Mr Joubert!' She pictured a man with silver hair in a white coat, leaning over her solicitously, 'Now then, what exactly is your problem, Mrs Hentze? Oh, I see. Well, a course of regular sessions and we'll soon change all that!'

'Just because I'm in the minority here, it doesn't make me a head case! If you were surrounded by the friends I had before I came to South Africa, you would be in the minority. And if they were here, they would feel isolated, too.'

[81]

Opinions of non-South Africans invariably irritated him. 'People who weren't born here don't understand this country. They feel free to criticise without knowing what they are talking about. It's pure arrogance on their part – that's your trouble, too, arrogance. But I'm warning you, Lilian, seriously, you will be stupid if you let these things affect our life together. What about the children, have you thought about them?'

Of course she thought about them, constantly; but that didn't mean ceasing to be a human being; on the contrary, with children, it seemed to her, the responsibility to live an example of common humanity was all the greater. This in fact was a major concern, and one more reason for avoiding the coffee mornings, for in the houses she had visited, she had been appalled by the behaviour of children to the black servants who cared for them and the thought that it might rub off on her own (peer influence being as strong as it is) was unacceptable. It was hard to believe it conceivable that young, innocent minds and hearts could treat with scorn and disdain the very people who fed them, bathed them, hugged them when they were sad or had hurt themselves; who smiled and laughed and told them their bedtime stories. Did they see them – following the example of their parents – merely in terms of someone to pick up their toys from the ground, to wash and iron their clothes, polish the floors, peel potatoes, clean, scrub, cook and always be on hand to fetch, carry, find lost things, forever smiling: Yes, madam! Yes, baas! Did all the love and kindness received mean nothing to them, nothing at all? Could children really be such monsters? It seemed they could, when they had parents who were so.

Gradually, as time passed, from within her wilderness of not knowing what this man, her husband, thought, believed, wanted or even expected from his existence – his inconsistencies making communication difficult, to say the least – she began to feel that his sudden irritations had less to do with her opinions than he would be prepared to admit. For although he would speak from whatever point of view he felt like at the time, some quite outrageous to her ear (no doubt for one reason or another, if only that of practising his strange and successful art of confusing people) by degrees it became obvious that he had no real objection to her way of doing things. He never, for example, showed disapproval or annoyance when children from the nearby settlement grew less timid and started to infiltrate the boundary hedges, or came up through the scrubland to play in the garden; he would greet them as he might greet any other friends of his children. And she wondered then, had he in fact wanted the obedient yes-woman type of wife he seemed to pretend to expect, for if that were really the case, he would have been too clever to choose a wife from her family, knowing as he did that in her home, obedience did not rate high on the list of moral priorities; her father had done hard labour for refusing to take part in the First World War, her grandfather had made himself unpopular denouncing the Boer War, and Lilian, although not a great thinker, had at least never been discouraged from thinking for herself.

But now, or rather of late, Lilian had come to be aware of a new role Carl seemed to be creating for himself, that of family man with a problematic home life; making a convincing show of having given up, shrugging helplessly and goodnaturedly to his friends, even in front of her, letting it be known that he had a difficult wife, what could he do? They smiled and pitied him, felt embarrassed for him if they visited and happened to catch sight of local Coloured children playing with his own in the garden, small black faces laughing up from the swimming pool. They would drive away uneasily, but not report it because after all it was not 'poor Carl's' fault. And it would never for a moment have occurred to them (any more than it did to Lilian) that 'poor Carl' was almost certainly laughing at them.

He had come back from sea. No reference was made to the question of the revolver (which was just as well since it was now buried somewhere out in the scrubland); instead he was full of the news of another course in the UK – Plymouth and then Portsmouth. His presence seemed to fill the house after his long absence; it was all plans, arrangements, organisation. Lilian was glad, too. In fact it was only when the possibility arose, became a reality instead of a dream, that she realised how deeply she longed to see her father, her friends, her country; to be among people who would not see her as an aberration in need of a psychologist; an outsider, a foreigner, the problematic wife of 'poor Carl'.

It was only many years after this time that she realised how useful she must have been to him, exactly the way she was. Visiting her and the children, living by then in Dublin – probably between other more important jaunts in Europe – he had been explaining one of his methods of getting through customs with minimum inspection. It was, he said, to make an almighty row over something stupid, like an outrageously large bottle of perfume, refuse to pay duty on it, lose his temper, give the officials a hard time, and then finally capitulate and get out the cheque book. According to him, they would be so relieved to get rid of him (and she could believe it) that they would barely bother to do more than a cursory glance at the passport, a hasty open and shut of the suitcases.

She had refrained from asking which of his nine passports he was using, but later on, when in idle conversation over remembered things and people in South Africa, he had come out with the startling remark, 'Anyway, thank God you weren't like those bitches!'

She had replied in amazement, trying to recollect who he could mean, 'What bitches?'

'The other naval wives.'

There followed a long silence before Lilian managed to say, 'But you were always on at me to be like them!'

He had smiled and said no more on the subject. That evening he left.

So all the alienation from society, the soul-searching, the concern for his position and feelings, the being cast as the difficult wife, all that had simply been useful for him, grist to his mill! Was it possible that her very loneliness and isolation had suited him, had provided the smokescreen he required, kept people occupied with gossip, and thus thrown the scent off his treasonable activities? Unfortunately, she was discovering that anything was possible.

They decided to rent out their house. Neither liked the prospect of another family living there – and they didn't need the money, all expenses would be covered abroad, plus generous overseas allowances – but they had been warned that to leave a house unoccupied in the South African countryside, even for six months (and they were to be away for two years) would bring disastrous consequences. Quite apart from the human element – vagrants might discover it, Noordhoek being an unpoliced area – the animal world would be certain to move in; sandfleas, baboons, deer, snakes, poisonous spiders and every other kind of insect. It wasn't to be considered. And the real advantage of renting out was that Harry and Teena could work on in guaranteed employment, and hopefully want to continue when the Hentze family returned. Lilian could not imagine the place without them. It struck her starkly that they were the only people she would miss; they and the young Irish nuns of the small convent school in Fishhoek, with whom she had gradually become friendly, exchanging a few words, swapping similar views on apartheid, each time she picked up the children. Being nuns though, they had not been permitted to make social visits, or accept invitations to her home. Only sometimes, when they had shopping and errands to do, she was allowed to give them a lift into Capetown and then they might just go for a cup of tea in some little place. As with Teena and Harry, it was a sort of friendship, but with artificial barriers.

On the last evening before they left, she stood out on the lawn, on the farthest point from the house, above the scrubland, her eyes searching the familiar scenery for some kind of hope, some kind of promise. The sea, autumnal, tenebrous and swollen from the storm of the night before, lay below; a huge expanse, hardly seeming to move, just heaving faintly as if emitting long sighs. For more than thirty hours waves had pounded the coastline, hurling dark seaweed across the usually radiant beach, so that this evening it looked almost black in the dwindling light, severe and sombre, as if in mourning.

It was strange to think it was spring in England. Devonshire would be all primroses, catkins, and new born lambs. And she would see the stars of the northern hemisphere once more, make out the remembered constellations. Her mind lingered pleasurably on things missed, soon to be embraced again; then shifted back to her present surroundings. She would miss this place, too, yes, despite the associated difficulties. She turned to look at the long building which had housed them during the past several years. In the deepening dusk the walls stood out white against the merging trees and grass; warm light from the windows lit the stoep, the hanging clumps of bougainvillea, and made bright streaks across the water in the fishpond. Drawn to the homely aspect and by the desire to be with her family, she was on the point of re-crossing the lawn when she saw Carl's tall form moving out of the shadows towards her.

'You're here then,' he said, coming up close and looking out to sea himself. 'Having a last look, eh?'

'Yes,' she replied. 'There'll hardly be time in the morning, there always seem to be last minute things to see to.'

'The trunks will already be on the ship now, in our cabins, waiting for us.' His voice sounded strained and his eyes roved the dark beach and valley below, in much the same way as her own had done earlier.

She felt intuitively that they both feared something, but that the 'something' was different for each; private thoughts, not to be shared. For him, perhaps he knew he would be moving into deeper waters; a new and more complicated phase of his extra-curricular activities. More would be expected of him.

Lilian's apprehensions were concerned only with the family. She had an ungrounded foreboding that the house would never look the same again – at least not in her eyes.

6

They rented a house on Dartmoor, just outside the village of Yelverton. From there Carl drove every day down to Plymouth; the first part of his course being a return to the Manadon Royal Naval Engineering College. It was practically home ground for Lilian, for she had grown up some twenty odd miles away, in a small town spread across the river Dart, and she knew the moors well from countless expeditions with her father, a Dartmoor enthusiast.

During the early part of her life, the family car, like all private cars in wartime, had been laid up on bricks in the garage, so outings had meant marathon events; her father, herself and her older sister taking their bikes (black-painted handlebars and wheelspokes according to regulations) on the local steam train to Ashburton, and then riding up onto the moors from there, packets of jam or Marmite sandwiches tied to the back carriers.

Devon, being all hills and valleys, was not the best

county for bicycle riding in those pre-multigear days; mostly it was a matter of lugging up the hills and free-wheeling down the other side, hoping the brakes would not give out. But since it was also one of the most breathtakingly beautiful counties, such considerations scarcely mattered and anyway, as her father used to say, 'What's wrong with a bit of effort?'

He had other things on his mind, too. He used to dis-appear into small isolated farms to see if there might be surplus produce to buy, and usually would reappear beaming and pleased, carrying a bag of eggs or handmade butter or cheese. At the same time the two children, being junior members of the Royal Society of British Wild Flowers, would have their own missions to complete; filling in postal questionnaires about flowers they found on the moors, giving detailed descriptions and the approx-imate locations. The highlight, however, would always be the same – the picnic and a swim in the river. For the Dart was everywhere, winding its way across the moors and down to the sea at Dartmouth. If it was hot they would find rocks, one each, flat granite slabs, mid-river, and lie stretched out on their backs, looking up at the sky through the overhanging branches of trees, or watching brightly coloured dragonflies, hearing, in the silence, the water flowing by on either side.

It wouldn't always be Dartmoor though, for they lived only six miles from the sea. Cycling to the coast, arriving hot and sticky, smelling the salt in the air, climbing through high coils of barbed wire – barricades against invasion –

onto the beach, and running at last into the blue-green waves, was yet another kind of magic.

The war was a mystery to Lilian. She heard the word mentioned from time to time, but no one had ever explained the meaning of it to her, and indeed she never asked. Only by stringing certain observations together did she form some sort of impression of her own. For example, if she was out walking in the country lanes with her nanny, and aeroplanes chanced to fly overhead, she would almost certainly be pushed into a ditch, and hear her nanny cry out in strangulated tones, 'The Jerries! Hide from the Jerries!' This she came to accept as normal, because she understood it was connected in some way to 'the war'. Or if the air raid warning sounded on the town siren, they would have to leave whatever they were doing, their beds if it was night time, and go to the air raid shelter, built in the house by her father, and he would read stories to them. If bombs dropped in the fields nearby and rattled the window panes (a rare occurrence) and her nanny started to panic, her father would say calmly, 'None of that, please,' and she would become calm, too, and behave normally again. The only really interesting thing about the war, as far as she could see, was that on occasion the empty roads became filled with long convoys of American army trucks, and usually, as they passed through the town, soldiers would be sitting out on top of the tank carriers, waving in a cheery way and throwing packets of sweets and chocolate down to the children for whom, in those rationed times, it appeared like manna from heaven.

Once Lilian and some friends had found a rabbit in a field, its leg trapped in a metal snare. Unable to open the jaws of the snare, they had run to a nearby road and discovered a convoy coming towards them. Jumping out in front of the first truck with cries of 'Stop!' and 'Help!' they had brought the long line of vehicles to a halt, and after some persuasion, the driver and his companion, carrying a box with a red cross on it, had followed them back across the field to where the rabbit lay. The way the two young men knelt beside the animal, released its leg and then, selecting instruments and bandages from their box, had bound it in a neat splint, impressed the children almost to the point of being speechless. 'Take him home, look after him for a week, then remove the bandage and let him go,' they were told. 'But be sure to bring him back here to the same spot you found him.'

With the rabbit, which had long ceased to struggle, they accompanied the soldiers back to the waiting convoy, and waved them off with cries and shouts of gratitude, unaware in their joy, that the convoy was almost certainly making its way to the coast for a night crossing to France, to join the front.

For Lilian, the end of the war was marked by the car coming out of the garage back onto its wheels after years off the ground, propped on bricks. This, of course, had meant more excursions, and further afield, and long walks now that energies were no longer expended on bicycle riding. The car, a 1927 Rolls-Royce, had a wooden dashboard, leather seats, cream-coloured silk curtains – slightly

moth eaten by now – which rolled up or down at the touch
of matching silk tassels, and a small oval-shaped
mahogany table in the back which, like a flap, could be put
up or down as required. It seemed enormous and old-fash-
ioned even then. Friends used to laugh at it and call it the
tank, but her father maintained it personally with loving
care; his great pride being the silence of the engine – its
approach virtually undetectable by human ear. He taught
Lilian to drive it when she was fifteen, taking her round
and round the disused racetrack on the edge of the town,
which had not seen a horse since before the war, until he
was satisfied with her, and after that on deserted parts of
Dartmoor. She passed her test in it when she was old
enough and had continued to drive it up to the time of her
marriage, or rather until she left for South Africa.

And South Africa seemed far now. The slow and easy
Devon pace had wrapped itself around her; the green hills
and valleys and deep dark rivers taking her back as if she
had never left, for her roots were there in the red soil. Every
week she drove across the moors to Totnes, her home
town, or her father would drive over to spend the day with
her. Mostly they sat and talked in the garden, but sometimes they would walk in the old favourite places and watch
the children dipping in the river – ghosts of her own past.
   Carl seemed satisfied with his course at Manadon.
There was much work to be done, covering new ground in
modern technology, and there would be exams, so he
spent a good deal of time away from home, studying in the

college library. There were social events, too, for the Royal Navy (unlike the less sophisticated South African Navy) never ceased its rounds of balls, dinners, cocktail parties and festivities of one kind or another. Carl was anxious about her wardrobe. 'I have things,' she said, but certainly made no objection when he pressed her to get more. They went together to a place which always had good clothes, and coming into the shop with her – a thing he had never done before – he sat smoking a cigar while she tried on ballgowns and dinner dresses, having her come out from the changing room and show him each one.

'Which shall I take? Which one do you like best?' she asked when she had finished.

'Take the lot,' he replied, with an expansive wave of his cigar, and the wistful-looking saleswoman had given a little clap of her hands, as if something had happened to cheer up her day.

He told Lilian he was having luck on the stock exchange; or rather not luck so much as good management, that anyone who used his brain could expect to make a second income on the side. As she was in no doubt as to his cerebral excellence – although his wisdom, she felt, was a different matter – she accepted his word without undue curiosity; the proof was there after all, for money appeared to be plentiful – naval couples of their age did not usually have such spacious rented accommodation or drive new Mercedes Benz cars. But this she had taken to be due to the extra overseas allowances allotted by the South African Navy.

Naturally enough, word of his financial wizardry began to circulate within Manadon and in due course other officers in his class started coming to him for advice, but not, it seemed, to any great or even notable success. Later on a new rumour found its circuitous way to Lilian's ears, that she herself, Carl's wife, was an heiress. And although initially she shook her head in disbelief and laughed at the extraordinary charge, believing that such a misconception could be dispatched with ease and speed, in time she discovered that she was up against an unsalvageable situation, for the rumour had come from Carl himself. Defeated (for how can you tell people your husband tells lies, or is merely fantasising?), she withdrew from the arena and concentrated on family life. If he wanted to tell people she was an heiress, let him. She just felt sorry he had the need, as she thought then, for self-aggrandisement.

Spring, summer, autumn; they had all passed leaving hardly a trace behind them, just pleasant memories, like a faint perfume. The winter was severe that year; snow lay all over Dartmoor; blizzard after blizzard covering old tracks and footprints, renewing the white landscape. From leaden skies helicopters dropped hay to half-submerged cattle, and food supplies to the isolated farms and village shops. It took Carl all of one day to drive from Yelverton to Manadon and, as there were no signs of a thaw, he decided to stay there in college until the end of the freeze-up, which in fact lasted over two weeks. In the house the water froze in the pipes, and the daily routine of melting snow in saucepans on the kitchen range took precedence over all else, the children helping to bring it in from the garden in buckets and basins. By the end of each day there was enough water for simple priorities, such as drinking, cooking, washing and flushing – and the next morning they would start all over again. As well as this there was the afternoon tramp to the shops around the village green and then tea by the fire in the drawing room when they got back. It was entirely enjoyable for they had nothing else to do, unlike those with businesses to run, or farmers unable to get to their cattle. As the snowbound conditions continued on into the second week, the general feeling in the village was of a weary exhaustion. Then one morning the world, or rather that small part of the world, awoke to clear skies and, if the sun was watery and weak, at least it gave out an incipient warmth. The diminishing snow, now reduced to patches, revealed expanses of grass, crushed but nevertheless green. The thaw had started and with it had come the sweet reprieve of spring. Touching, the joy of the children when they saw the car in the drive, 'Look! Daddy's back!'

Portsmouth loomed next on the agenda. Carl went on up to enrol in the naval establishment there, and after fruitless attempts to find a house to rent, they decided that Lilian and the children should stay in Devon with her father – who lived alone, with a daily housekeeper coming in – and Carl himself would drive down on Friday evenings and return late on Sundays. He again had a lot of work to get through, and would prefer to concentrate on it during the week and then have the weekends free, away from Portsmouth, to be with his family. For her part, Lilian was tired of mixing in naval circles, pre-typecast by Carl (which put her straight away on a false footing) as his 'Danish' wife, or 'difficult' wife, or 'heiress' wife; never knowing what might come next. Anyway, social gatherings with captains' wives where hats and gloves were worn, the conversation polite and stilted, wasn't her style. She also preferred the alternative arrangement.

There was a mews flat over the stables. It had been an apple loft once, spanning the stables, harness room and what had originally been a coach house but was now the garage. Lilian's father had made the conversion during the early years of the war, to provide refuge for evacuee families. Now it made an ideal temporary home, preferable to living in the house, for as soon as her father (elderly now, and accustomed to a quiet and solitary existence) showed signs of becoming tired, she could immediately withdraw with the children, leaving him his own space.

Familiar surroundings, familiar faces in the shops and high street, familiar comments, such as: 'I remember you when you were a little maid, and used to ride your pony through the town.' Friends were gone; married and left home, but there were parents to visit, old times to be recalled. The children attended the kindergarten class of her old school, and some of the teachers from her day were still there: 'I knew your mummy when she was no bigger than you are. She used to sit in that very desk there!'

'Tell us, tell us!' her children would wheedle, wanting to hear stories about her. 'Was she naughty?'

And all they could elicit would be a tantalising, 'Ah . . .'

In retrospect, from a distance of a decade or even two, Lilian was always inclined to look back in gratitude on this year – unexpectedly given her, out of the normal course of events – as very important in her life. For without it she might never have had the opportunity to get to know her father over a prolonged period, as one adult to another; to see the person she had previously only looked at through the often critical eyes of an adolescent, and to become so much the richer for it.

He had been forty-three when she was born, and although this age-gap gave a formality to the relationship, it by no means hindered or inhibited it. For Lilian, as early as she could remember, he was a father who communicated openly and directly, listened with grave respect to whoever addressed him, child or adult, and was always willing to talk about whatever you wanted; nothing was ever too serious or too trivial. His readiness for fun and laughter had obscured his social isolation, to the point that it never occurred to her. The fact that he was always alone, reading in various languages, gardening, playing the piano, she had blithely assumed to be simply his nature, the way he liked to live his life.

The truth, she came to realise later, was that there, in the thick of the Devon countryside he loved so well, he was not even a square peg in a round hole – no slot of any shape existed for him. He hated the class distinctions rife at that time, and the type of socialising that was expected of him, not to mention the general assumption that one should approve of blood sports, and the affront inevitably aroused by contradictory opinions. He knew he was considered to be uncomfortable company, but was unable to pretend to views he had not. He was revolted by the spectacle of people dressing up in special clothes in order to make a sport of chasing, terrorising and killing an animal. If it had to be destroyed, he would say, let at least the job be done with sorrow, as an unpleasant necessity, not as an event to be enjoyed.

A lonely and passionate man, he was accustomed to exclusion. He had known the wounds of disillusionment, disappointment and betrayal, and come to terms with them. Only the seventh in England to refuse to fight in the 1914 war, scarcely more than a boy at the time, just down from Cambridge with a degree in civil engineering, he had declined to have a lawyer for his trial. 'I will not take orders from anyone,' he had said, 'to kill another man. You can send me anywhere you like, you can put a gun in my hand, but you can't make me fire it.'

Afterwards the judge who had sentenced him, had shaken him by the hand and expressed a bemused kind of sympathy.

He was put first in Warwick Prison. He found an irony in being placed among murderers and wrote to the authorities asking them to make up their minds: should a man be imprisoned for murder, or for refusing to murder? To punish both seemed ridiculous. Later he was moved, with other conscientious objectors as the numbers increased, to Dartmoor Prison.

His family turned their backs in shame, he was no longer considered a son. He had, however, no regrets. Dartmoor Prison, he told Lilian, had been his real university. Here he had learned to break slate in the quarries, from dawn to dusk, in every weather; to walk in chains and have feathers, symbolising cowardice, thrown at him; to eat porridge three times a day; to live with all sorts from all walks, and yet had discovered himself to be in more congenial company than at any other time in his life – which hitherto had consisted of a boarding preparatory school from the age of six, then Winchester College, and then Cambridge. Disliking equally authoritarianism and fanaticism of all kinds, he believed firmly in the right to be responsible for oneself. Later in his life he had found himself also responsible for two small girls, aged six and three, and had done his best to make a home for them.

'Tell me something,' Lilian said to him, in one of their idle conversations; they were sitting together, not talking about anything in particular, 'I've always wanted to know . . .?'

'What have you always wanted to know?'

'What you lived on, all through the war? I've often thought about it. I only remember that you divided all the rationed foods between us children. Never touched any of it yourself. So what on earth did you eat all those years?'

'What nonsense! There were plenty of other things to eat.'

'I asked you once, why you didn't eat butter, or meat, or all the things we were eating, and you said you didn't like them. You said you thought they were boring. I thought it really odd.'

'You've got children of your own,' he said. 'What would you do?'

'What else could I do now, after your example?' And to tease him she added, 'And you did black market deals, too, didn't you? Swapped your tea rations?'

'Only with people who hadn't got children. They preferred tea to butter and eggs. And you know, we always had fruit and vegetables.'

She had been too young to remember him digging up the lawns and flowerbeds, laying out vegetable gardens, putting in raspberry canes, strawberries, gooseberries, currants, but she could still see him standing out there, hoeing the earth between rows of cabbages or spinach or carrots or onions, or tying up the peas and beans. So good and patient always.

'I'll never forget the asparagus,' she said, 'eating it freshly picked, with melted butter.'

'We were very fortunate to have the ground. And the orchard, with the plums and apples and cob nuts.'

'And the tomatoes,' she added, 'in the greenhouse. I loved going in there; I loved the smell.'

The house had been unlived in for some time before her father had bought it, and rats had moved into the garden.

'Do you remember the rats?' he said. 'The way they used to come up from the garden and sit in a row under the drawing room window whenever I played the piano? I felt really sorry having to get rid of them. There was something touching about rats who liked listening to Bach!'

His views on child-rearing were entirely his own, and possibly eccentric. While on the one hand he brooked no argument concerning good manners, for the rest he believed in what he called 'healthy neglect' and no children could have had more freedom to roam the surrounding country on ponyback or on foot, with friends or on their own. But the home was never empty, there was always the security of his presence.

As always when a routine of some sort is established, time passed almost unnoticed. Carl continued to come and go at weekends, carrying, seemingly, a burden of preoccupation. Lilian perceived the change in him and even her father, who would normally never comment, observed – after witnessing some outburst of irritability – that it must be an extremely arduous course he was doing.

She suggested that maybe it was too much, driving down every Friday after a week's work. Would he prefer to spend some weekends up in Portsmouth, just resting? His vehemence surprised her: he would not, it appeared, not at all.

It was hardly the right time to have to announce that she was pregnant, but the fact existed and, although totally unexpected, from the moment of realisation, there was for her that familiar deep thrill that a new life had begun in her.

'I can't have another child at this stage in my life,' he shouted. 'It doesn't fit in with my plans!'

'What plans?'

'You'll have to have an abortion!'

Seeing on his face that her feelings would be of no account, she said, clutching at straws, 'It's illegal!'

'Not in Sweden. You'll have to go to Sweden and have it done there.'

'I certainly will not!'

'I order you to!' He hit the table with his fist.

'You can order all you like,' she said, and rising, removed herself from the presence which had suddenly become unbearable to her.

She didn't dwell on Carl's reaction after he had left, coldly annoyed, that weekend. She knew her father had two Achilles' heels, and that she was one of them. Because he could not bear her to be hurt, she could not bring her hurt to him. Therefore life continued much as before on the surface, as if nothing untoward had happened, and if she grieved privately, she was nevertheless happy in her fiercely protective love for the unborn child; happy in the discovery that where there is real joy, nothing can dim it.

She felt sorry for Carl in a way – not entirely, for she was feeling wounded – but she sensed he was in some difficulty of his own that he did not wish to share. And she believed, too, that it was his right to tell or not, as he saw fit; she believed in everyone having his or her own space, the right to be trusted. Whatever it was, he was clearly under pressure of one sort or another and didn't want another baby in the home, another child to rear, and – not believing that life is sacred – abortion was the obvious answer for him. But what if you believe, as she did, that life *is* sacred? That the foetus is a live human being with already its own nature, its own soul? Then abortion cannot be even contemplated. And what to do when there were these two conflicting and opposite viewpoints, neither so much a matter of wrong or right, but of what you believed, for here there could be no compromise, no middle road, no meeting ground or halfway house – it was Yes or No. Lilian, whose body was the guardian of the unborn child, had said No and Carl, after all, could not force her.

It was in these uneasy circumstances that they prepared to return to their home in South Africa.

It was a sombre leaving. The coming of spring had been frustrated that year by late frosts, mean winds and a lack of rain. Growth had been inhibited, the budding stalled. The Cornish coast still had a wintry aspect as the liner steamed down the grey-green smudgy waters of the Channel and took its final departure from Scilly's lighthouse.

As, traditionally, evening dress is not worn on either the first or last night at sea, Lilian and Carl, in woollens and tweeds of much the same hue as the dreary landscape they had just left behind, sat in the lounge over after-dinner coffees, surveying the other passengers (who looked unpromisingly staid) and tried to convince each other they were enjoying themselves. Unaware they were heading towards a gale in the Bay of Biscay, and both suffering from lacklustre spirits, they shared a dread of the days spread out ahead of them; a dread of boredom, cooped together with little to say.

The first sign of the storm was a strange motion of the ship, a sort of sudden sideways shift, a quiver that ran through her structure from end to end, causing people to stumble and almost lose their footing. This happened about the second day out. Carl, feeling under his feet the uneasiness of the ship, and recognising the motion, emerged from the lethargy in which he had taken refuge, and told Lilian to be prepared for what was coming. 'It should be interesting,' he said, 'but nothing to worry about. These ships can withstand anything.'

The next morning the ship was rolling steadily. A dense band of cloud covered the sun, letting through only lurid coppery rays of light. The air was heavy. At midday, winds arose and bursts of lightning illuminated the great waste of broken seas. Raindrops spattered the decks and although it was obvious they were running into a storm, there was nothing to indicate the viciousness of the first squall when it came; the startling fury, passion and wrath of the attack.

They watched, through reinforced glass at the side of the deck, the water going up and up in a sheer face, like some living creature with a mind of its own, then topple and come sliding down again, subsiding in a great rush of foaming crests. And the huge liner would pitch forward, seeming to rise clean out of the sea before lurching down into the dark hollows, yawning and empty, beneath the running walls of water. Above the tearing winds, the unappeasable crashing of the sea, the driving sheets of rain, a shrill whistling could be heard, which seemed to issue from some vast, obscure, uncharted place.

None of the Hentze family got seasick; rather each appeared exhilarated, ebullient even. It is said there is nothing like an encounter with the elements, a confrontation with natural powers, for bringing us face to face with our smallness, our insignificance; Lilian, on the contrary, was moved to feel twice the woman she normally considered herself to be – no longer a person of everyday tasks, petty successes and petty failures, but an amazon, privileged to be a part of so diverse, so glorious and magnificent a world. And long after the abatement, when all was serene once more, an expanse of radiant blue opening up to them, it became evident that Carl had left behind the pressures he had been carrying; simply cast them off like a snake its old skin. He looked a new man, or rather the Carl of past times; the tenseness and irritability gone from his face. The children sensed it first, as children do, and then Lilian, too, seeing him relaxed and joking (when he was like that there was no better company), gave herself up to the pleasure of enjoying the rest of the sea voyage all together as a family.

On the Southampton to Capetown run, the Castle Line ships usually called in at one or other of the Canary Islands. This time it dropped anchor in the bay of the Grand Canary, and was instantly surrounded by boats and rafts of all sizes and shapes; women holding up lace tablecloths and local handcrafts; youths and young men – and a few older men with brown wiry bodies – diving for coins; and altogether a mêlée of shouting, bargaining, quarrelling and laughter. Motor-boats ferried passengers to the port, from where they could take a car or pony and trap and explore the countryside or, alternatively, stay among the shops and restaurants around the harbour.

The Hentzes found a horse-drawn cab and made for the nearby hills, the children taking turns to sit with the driver and hold the reins. They had a meal somewhere above the town, on a shaded terrace overlooking the vast Atlantic Ocean and the almost toy-like bay, now dominated by the great silver liner. It was one of those good times when they all laughed until they cried about nothing at all, and the whole of creation seemed to have been invented purely for their pleasure. The horsecab driver, seated at another table and also enjoying a simple meal, and the horse, tied nearby, munching grass, both needed some persuasion to forego a siesta and get them back to the port in order to catch the returning motor ferries. But in fact they knew better, for there was plenty of time and to spare.

On a long sea journey it is possible to feel not only attached to your ship, but also quite dependent on it. Re-embarking had been like coming home; the cabins, which had been locked all day because of the influx of strangers on board, were unlocked, the anchors hoisted, dinner served, and routine went thankfully back to normal.

The end of that sea voyage was the end of an era; their lives (Carl would have known it, but Lilian had no notion) were never to be the same again.

7

The house, larger than she had remembered, stood deserted and uncared for; autumn leaves piled against the locked doors, windows caked with sand, a few panes cracked or missing. The garden, however, was immaculate; flowerbeds and lawns well-watered, and signs of work done recently in the vegetable garden. They opened up all the doors and french windows, took brooms and swept the whole place out; disrupting as they did so, the sleep of one snake and several lizards, which fled, and a variety of nasty-looking insects which showed more reluctance at being budged. Then they put clean sheets on the beds, made a meal of vegetables from the garden, and spent their first night at home being half eaten to death by fleas.

In the morning Harry knocked on the french windows to the dining room while they were having breakfast.

'Morning, baas! Morning, madam!'

'Harry!' The children shouted his name gladly and ran to him.

He stood smiling down at them as they tugged at his hands, and declined an offer of coffee, 'No thanks, baas.' But after answering the children's questions about their pony and Lilian's horse, which were being looked after by neighbours, he came and sat at the breakfast table, first removing his gardening hat and carefully wiping the soles of his shoes on the outside mat.

The tenants, he told them, had left early, unexpectedly, two and a half months ago. The husband's ship had left Capetown ahead of schedule (it was a Royal Navy ship) and the family had simply packed up and left, gone back to England, without notifying the house agent or arranging for anyone to caretake – just gone, ignoring their contract, ignoring their obligations.

Had they paid Harry? For the months they had left him alone?

'No, baas, but I knew you'd put things right, so I just carried on.'

And Teena?

'Ah . . . Teena, madam. She went. She got married and she went.'

Teena's man friend, who used to visit some weekends, had got promotion where he worked in the Forestry Commission up in the mountains. He was foreman now, with his own house, and Teena, the baby and Elsie, had gone up to live with him. That was a year ago.

Glad, suppressing her selfish sorrow at losing her, Lilian

acknowledged the news as the best possible. She had been convinced, when the man used to come to stay, that he was a really good person; Teena, above all, deserved the best.

There was a pile of mail waiting to be opened. Fraught by the amount of things to be done; the unpacking, shopping, cooking and cleaning, Lilian turned instead to the letters, picking through to read the interesting ones first. Some of them were quite old, dating back to soon after they had gone overseas; they had been left to accumulate in an untidy heap. She read a couple through, and then noticed one addressed to them both, in handwriting she couldn't place. She was sure she had never seen it before. The postmark was England. Carl was unpacking and hanging his uniforms when she went to find him.

'Do you remember Robert McDaid?'

'Of course.'

'There's a letter to us both from his sister in England, in Kent. She says he committed suicide.'

'Robert McDaid! Are you sure?' Carl's face scarcely moved. Then he asked, almost curtly, 'Why are you crying? You didn't know him well.'

'I just remember he always seemed so lonely and sad. His sister says they found him under his car in the garage – you know . . . with the exhaust on.'

'Stupid thing to do. How did the sister know about us? How did she know our address?'

'She said she got it off a Christmas card. I sent him one every year from both of us, he was on the list.'

'Well, that's that then, isn't it,' Carl said, turning back to his trunk, 'you won't have to send him any more Christmas cards.'

'She said he was home on leave, whatever that means – he wasn't in the navy was he? I thought he was some sort of business man. And she said that she and the family couldn't understand it, he seemed so happy and carefree. The strange thing is though, she said it was a pity he had never married! I thought the reason he was so depressed was his divorce. What do you make of that?'

'Nothing!' Carl said. 'And I've really heard enough on the subject. It doesn't help anyone to go on like that. Why don't you go and do something useful? What was that Harry said about knowing a woman who wants to work for us – take Teena's place?'

'She's coming this afternoon.' She felt sorry for Carl. Men were not supposed to show their feelings, they had to be manly, but inside he must be feeling awful. He had been a close friend of Robert's. She remembered their late phone conversations . . . 'Just for an interview. She lives somewhere nearby, here in Noorhoek.' She started to walk away, feeling flat.

'And cheer up,' Carl added, as she passed through the door. It sounded like an order and remained in her ears as she went along the passage to the kitchen.

Oh Teena, I miss you, I miss your warm smile! She remembered how they used to feed their children together around the kitchen table, laughing (they had always laughed together); Teena teaching her words and sentences from her language, Xhosa, the click language, almost impossible to pronounce for someone not born to it, and she thought: it's those small moments that make life good, not the big things.

And the burden of guilt came back to her; how could she live in this country, knowing that people like Teena and her children would never have the same rights to dignity and opportunity as she, Lilian, and her children!

Caroline also had a baby on her back, and Lilian was glad. She was not Bantu, like Teena, but a Coloured woman, with wavy hair framing her face and a smile nobody could see and not feel the better for. Probably in her late twenties, Lilian thought, around the same age as herself. Caroline's views on marriage were jaundiced, to say the least: 'No, madam, not me,' she said, tilting her head and laughing at the very idea. 'Me – my boyfriend is a good man, he gives me presents and treats me well. And the money I earn is my own. When you marry, they beat you, take your money and spend it on other women. That's not for me, madam. I'm too clever for that!'

And yes, she indeed looked far too clever for that, but kind too; Lilian liked her instantly. She suggested waiting until after the weekend, so that Harry could paint out the little flat, but Caroline was dismissive. 'Get the baas to bring some paint,' she said, 'and I'll do it myself. I want to.' And in no time she was in there, singing, cleaning, painting; making the rooms neat and pretty, like herself.

No one would have been aware of the support the

young Coloured woman gave to Lilian through those last months of pregnancy, her empathy during Lilian's growing incertitude at that time. It was not merely the return of Carl's tenseness, the outbursts of annoyance for no apparent reason, that caused her unease. Now there were graver indications that something was really wrong. It is, after all, somewhat unnerving when the person you feel a certain dependence on, starts showing serious signs of irrationality, and as Lilian's spirits eroded, Caroline's quick eyes saw and understood and conveyed many things. Outside the home, however, there was nobody to observe and support. Who on earth would believe the things Lilian could describe? In the supermarket, for example: she herself, list in hand, loading a trolley while Carl browsed the shelves further off for extra items of his choice – what could be more normal? But then suddenly he was at her side, saying with a strained tone to his voice: 'Come on, we've got to go – now!'

'Yes, all right, I'm almost finished.'

'Don't argue, for Christ's sake, just do as you are told for once!'

Leaving the half-filled trolley in the aisle, they walked out and went to the car park. Sitting beside him on the way home, she waited for an explanation. When none was forthcoming, she said angrily, 'What the hell was that all about then?'

But the stonelike set of his face made it clear he had no intention of replying. He couldn't be right in the head! He must be ill, but she knew he would never admit it. To

whom could she go for help? The naval doctor? Or, iron-
ically, the Mr Joubert he had threatened her with? On the
other hand, she couldn't risk doing something that might
harm him – she wanted to help, not destroy his career.

Another time he started changing his clothes while
driving at high speed, snatching things from the back seat
with his free hand, pulling them over his head, muttering
that someone had recognised him – not so much ignoring
Lilian's protests, it was more as if her presence did not
exist – while she sat shaking her head in disbelief, furious
to have not just her own life, but the life of her unborn
child, and the welfare of her children waiting for her at
home, put at risk over some incomprehensible, half-witted
whim of his.

History was repeating itself. Again some neighbours,
white women, came to point out that she was spoiling
Caroline.

'Caroline?' Lilian said, 'I'm afraid it's the other way
round. Perhaps you should scold Caroline for spoiling me.'

They were not to be diverted. Their servants, they said,
were complaining about Caroline, because she always had
money, was always well-dressed.

'I don't think it's Caroline they are complaining about,'
Lilian said. 'They all like her.'

'They are envious of her, they never stop harping on
about her.'

'Is that a reason why she should not have nice clothes?
Perhaps there could be another solution?'

Then the usual: 'You aren't doing her a favour – or your-self! She won't appreciate what you give her, and she won't appreciate you. She'll laugh at you behind your back for being weak!'

'One time, when I was sick,' Lilian would reply, not hotly, but hoping that even one person might eventually listen, 'Caroline put me to bed and treated me like a princess, bringing me specially cooked omelettes and invalid soups. The local district nurse, doing her rounds, dropped in (I thought to see me) and asked how Caroline was. Caroline! Was something wrong with Caroline? "She is seriously ill," the district nurse told me reprovingly, how come I didn't know? We went together to her room and there she was, lying on her bed, crying from stomach pain. We had to get her into hospital that day. She hadn't wanted to say anything until she was sure I was better.'

Miraculously, nature being what it is, as the time for Lilian's confinement approached, she stopped worrying about Carl, lost interest in his peculiarities and bouts of insane behaviour, ceased to be concerned about anything except the business in hand. Some biological mechanism now dictated her mood; only one theme occupied her days – Life, the affirmation of Life. Everything was prepared and made ready; the rooms of the house as well as the occu-pants waited in a state of expectant repose. She felt she could almost hear the clocks ticking.

The time came. It's one thing, Lilian reflected, to 'see a world in a grain of sand, and a heaven in a wild flower', but what a mother beholds in the face of her newly born, in that first long look, surpasses all description. Carl just had time to see the baby before going to sea; his ship left Simonstown the day after he brought Lilian back from the hospital.

Part Two

◆

8

When people asked, as they often did, what had made Lilian choose Ireland as her place of refuge, her new country, her home, she found it hard to give a short and comprehensive answer. The obvious choice would have been to go back to Devon, but when you are wounded, it is very hard to return to the place where you have been happy, and to have people asking questions that are not only painful, but which you are not in a position to answer truthfully. The years as a naval wife had accustomed her to turning up in strange places, renting accommodation, settling herself and her children into new surroundings, and she felt at this point it was what she wanted to do; start a new life with her children.

After the discussions with Carl, culminating in her refusal to become his spy partner, they had talked about where she should go to live. Another part of England? Somewhere English-speaking anyway, and not too far from Devon, so that she could go back for frequent holidays. Whether he had first suggested Ireland, or she, she never noticed, but certainly she had always wanted to visit (twice she had planned holidays there, which had fallen through) and now seemed a good opportunity to discover if this calling to her of another country had any substance. She had only a hazy idea that it would be a green and gentle place and, according to newspaper reports, the problem of school children taking drugs had not yet crossed the Irish Sea. As a single parent now, she believed it might be an easier environment to give her children the simple and unprecocious childhood she had had herself.

It had not occurred to her at the time that from Carl's point of view, it must have been an ideal choice, Ireland being particularly exposed to all forms of international crime, used by criminals as a gateway to and from the rest of Europe. Only years later did she wonder if he had not perhaps had more of a hand in her decision than she had realised.

Arriving off the boat in Southampton, Lilian had first made her way down to Devonshire. She had wired her father to tell him she was on her way, giving the date of her arrival, but no explanation.

'How long will you be away from South Africa?' he had asked, after about two days, guessing something was wrong.

'For good,' was all Lilian had replied, with pain in her eyes.

'Splendid!' he said. He didn't mean it was splendid, of course, he simply wanted to convey his support and show that he was not going to ask questions; she could tell him what she wanted, when she wanted.

It was her first realisation of the isolation she had been cast into; she would never again be able to talk openly to friends or the people she loved. Always there would be a barrier, for they would know she was holding back, not confiding in them, and their feelings would be hurt. But she couldn't confide, never again, no matter how heavy the weight on her mind, or on her heart; she longed to and she could not, not even to her father, the one person in the world who really cared about her. And she owed it to him not to shut herself away, not to rebuff him, but she could do nothing about it. In his mid-seventies now, he was inclined to worry excessively about things, especially to do with his children, and if she were to explain that Carl had tried to recruit her to work for the Russians, that espionage was his real work, the navy his cover, he would never again sleep a night through. More serious perhaps, his memory was no longer reliable; he often couldn't remember what he said, or to whom, and because any of Lilian's revelations would be so much on his mind, he might easily go talking around the town, without realising it or forgetfully overlooking the paramountcy of secrecy. Lilian would never forget Carl's terrifying words about men appearing and putting plastic bags over the heads of children until they turned purple in the face to make mothers or members of the family talk. If the mother, he had said, didn't have the information they wanted, God knows what might happen. And in the case of her father, God knows what they might do to him, too. It was unbearable, quite unthinkable that she could put him to such risk by confiding in him. Whether she liked it or not, she had no option but to endure the sorrow and questioning in his eyes, and her own loneliness. And even then, none of them was safe.

And naturally enough at that time, there were also the inevitable speculations of neighbours and acquaintances, which circulated in her home town before coming to her ears; that she had got bored with her life in South Africa, or darker hints of a 'third party'. She was glad to leave, to take her children and go to make a fresh start, to find anonymity in new unknown territory.

In the estate agent's office, a large dusty room with dark green walls, somewhere in the city centre, she was asked by a man wearing an eyeshade, who looked more like a croupier than a man selling houses, which part of Dublin she would prefer to rent a flat in. Replying that she hadn't the faintest idea, that she didn't know Dublin, had never been in Ireland before, she was struck by the enormity of her situation – what was she doing here? However, she had started the ball rolling, and a list was produced. There was an unfurnished flat for five pounds a week. It was the cheapest on the list. 'I'll take that,' she said.

The agent looked in a file and then told her apologetically that it was gone, it had been taken that morning. She looked again. The next cheapest was for rent at five pounds and ten shillings. 'That one then,' she said.

On receipt of a month's rent she was given the keys, and the following day, with her children, she moved from the guest house they were staying in to their new home. The flat turned out to be in a terraced building, part of an early Victorian square, with a large park of overgrown grass in the middle, surrounded by black iron railings and colossal chestnut trees. There was an airy, high-ceilinged sitting room with a wide bay window and a white marble fireplace with proportions that told of grander days; two bedrooms partitioned by walls no thicker than plywood; a window-less kitchen that was more like a cupboard, with a few food-stained shelves and a filth-encrusted gas cooker; a draughty bathroom with window-frames that didn't fit, and a clogged up gas heater for the water. The floors were bare wooden boards, some loose, the cracks filled with ancient grime.

Daunted by the dirt and unfamiliar smells, the confining, cupboard-like rooms, she took the only line open to her – to pretend to the children that it was all great fun. Earlier in the day she had gone to a big store in O'Connell Street and bought camp beds, a cot for the baby, blankets and sheets, one kettle, one saucepan, one frying pan, an iron and ironing board, and a variety of cleaning things. She had arranged to have them delivered that afternoon, and as soon as they arrived she set to in a kind of desperation and scrubbed the whole place out, through and through. Time became blurred, merged into rounds of cleaning, shopping from a little corner shop at the far end of the park, cooking, washing and settling the children. The park was a blessing, they could sit out together on rugs, as if it were their own garden, and have stories and games.

About the fifth day, the landlord, a small, suave man with silver-grey hair and friendly open manner, called to introduce himself and enquire if everything was in order. Shocked to learn that Lilian knew no one in Dublin, in Ireland even, he disappeared, to return later with a woman, a mother also of young children, who lived in the same terrace. 'I couldn't leave you like that,' he said, 'not knowing a soul. Now you can make a start.'

And certainly, in only a matter of weeks – Irish people being what they are – Lilian and her children felt themselves becoming integrated into the community of that small neighbourhood. And when some bits and pieces of furniture, books, and the children's toys and personal belongings arrived, it was possible at last to start looking upon the flat as their home. There were still moments from time to time of almost physical pain when dismal thoughts would press in on her, but overall was a great sense of relief, and even of achievement, that she had got her children away from a menacing situation. Some mornings she would stand at the bay window, the baby in her arms, watching the children doing the milkround with the elderly milkman, who still used a horse and cart for his deliveries – or playing in the park, climbing the trees for conkers – and offer up heartfelt thanks for the peace of their new life.

And new life it was, a revelation in many aspects; for only now was it revealed to Lilian just how cushioned, how cocooned her previous existence had been. Never having travelled any way but first class, she was learning what it means to walk to save bus fares, to transport something heavy like a bag of potatoes or a sack of coal in a push chair, or on the saddle of an old bike. She had seen people doing such things, the way she had seen people standing in bus queues in the rain after a day's work, without wondering what it is like, day after day for a lifetime. And it came to her, too, how easily she had taken for granted the kind of domestic arrangements she had been accustomed to. Now, with no help, not even a washing machine, she found it necessary to plan her day around the never-ending cycle of household chores – that is if she wanted to avoid getting bogged down by them – doing such things as the ironing and peeling the vegetables in the evenings while the children were alseep. The washing, particularly the nappies, she left to soak overnight so that she could have them done and out on the line in the tiny strip of garden (more like a junk heap) at the back of the building early each morning. She found that if she stuck to a routine she could manage well enough, while to ignore it was at her peril, for she would become overwhelmed, exhausted and depressed. So it was that from being a person who had rather carelessly despised organisation, she came to see it instead as a means to freedom, to having time for herself, for all of them together.

Another facet of the new life was the locality – Dun

Laoghaire, a southern suburb, on the sea, close by the mountains. How it was that purely by chance, through choosing the cheapest flat on the house agent's list, they had arrived to live in what had turned out to be, in Lilian's view, quite the most congenial area of Dublin, remained one of those inexplicable mysteries our lives are punctuated with. The square too, Crosthwaite Park, was very much to her taste, mostly because of the sort of people who lived there, individuals all, kindhearted and friendly, many of them parents also with children going to the small school nearby. Certainly there was no lack of children in the neighbourhood, plenty in the square alone, and since the young have their own definite and direct ways of communication, friendships were soon formed. For herself, the best of Dun Laoghaire was in the long stretch by the sea and down around the harbour where yachts and fishing boats lay moored and passenger ferries left daily for Holyhead in Wales. She would walk there in the mornings, with the baby in the push chair, and look far out to sea, the way she had done when she used to ride her horse on the beach in South Africa, always looking for some kind of answer to the muddle and complexity of life, as if it existed out on the horizon somewhere, just out of reach. Slowly, apart from her own personal sadness, which she kept to herself, daily life took on a pleasant shape – and indeed all the pleasanter when they got into the practice of returning to Devon for the school holidays. To the children, their grandfather's house was now home from home, giving that extra security they needed; the man himself providing a role model of all that was decent, reasonable, kind and thoughtful, while for Lilian it was a place where time stood still, a place where childhood, adulthood and motherhood were all one.

During one of these visits Lilian felt obliged to mention her impending divorce to her father, reluctantly, knowing the subject saddened him. As always when something affected her deeply, she spoke casually, a feeling of constriction in her chest, 'The divorce papers will be coming soon. Apparently I only have to sign and return them – no court case or anything.'

'I see,' was all he said, and she couldn't look at him. After a while he added sorrowfully, 'I'm really sorry. I always thought you were an ideal family.'

'You never can tell,' was all she could think of to say.

'Couldn't you . . .' he was looking at her intently now, but with hesitation, not wishing to intrude.

'Couldn't I what?'

'Well . . . couldn't you perhaps be a little more forgiving . . . about whatever was wrong?'

She never came nearer to breaking down and telling everything than at that moment. He thought her unforgiving! He, whose opinion mattered to her more than anyone's. Unforgiving! It was one of the most painful moments of her life. She tried to hold him with her eyes, to convey something. 'All I can do is ask you to trust me,' she said, but not, she felt, convincingly. Why should he trust her, after all, when to him it must appear that she didn't trust him enough to open her heart? 'Please just trust me that I'm doing what I think right.'

'Yes,' he said, 'of course.'

That evening the whistle of a train in the valley below reminded her sharply of how when she was young, lying in her bed on summer evenings with her windows wide open, letting in the warm, wisteria-scented air, that same sound, that same shrill whistle in the night, redolent of adventure, of loneliness, of far off places, used to move her almost to a physical ache, almost to tears, as if it were telling her something about her future life which she intuitively knew, but did not want to accept. These trains, passing through the local station and along by the river, steam rising above the houses and trees, had been for her the only real indication that a world existed outside her home town and the surrounding countryside. They never, as a family, went away for holidays and Lilian did not remember having wished to do so. In fact she had turned down invitations from friends to go with them, for everything she liked was right there; it was her soil, she had grown there, learning to swim in the dark river, later riding her horse along its banks in all seasons, all weathers, most memorably in the early mornings with mists rising off the water and, if you were lucky, the silver flash of a salmon leaping. As a child she had played in the fields, helped (or believed she helped) at harvest times; standing up with other children on the horse-drawn hay wagons, afterwards being invited to join the farming families as they sat under the trees with their large kettles of tea and picnic baskets. She had belonged. Then she had gone away to college in Hertfordshire, and she had travelled and things had been sometimes good and sometimes bad, but they had never been the same again. Yes, it was true, there is no stepping in the same water twice; there is no going back.

She wondered then about Carl, had he ever wanted to go back, to the time before he had been recruited, to re-make his decision? She felt an intense sadness, for he had been so young when they got their hands on him; according to what he had told her, it was before they were married – he must have been twenty or twenty-one – very likely thinking it a bit of a lark. Had he felt scared when he first realised, as he must have done at some point, that he was trapped; that things were expected or demanded of him that maybe he did not want to do, and that there was no way out, ever? She wondered, too, about his mother, the anguish she would feel if she knew. She was so proud of his success in the navy, so ambitious for him, so sure of him.

She thought that night she would never sleep and, when she did, she dreamed that a person whose face she could not see was firing a rifle and dead or wounded birds were dropping from the sky.

The lawyer's office in Dublin was all bookshelves, heavy furniture and dark curtains, solemn and reassuring, and the man himself, smiling at her with warm, sensitive eyes, was doing his best to make her feel at ease. 'It's just a matter of signing your name,' he said, 'and it's all over.'

Imagine that! You simply sign your name and all the years of your marriage, everything it contained – the love, the laughter, the tears, the children – it's all over! 'Yes,' she said. 'Of course.'

'I have the document from South Africa,' he pushed it across the desk to her. 'You'd better read it through before you sign.'

'Yes,' she said again, and took the pen he offered. Her hand had begun to shake.

At that time, for a divorce to be arranged, someone had to be at fault; there had to be a guilty party and an innocent party. Carl and his South African lawyer had decided that Lilian was to be the guilty party.

'Wait a minute,' she objected, when she had finished reading. 'It says I "wilfully and maliciously" packed my bags, took the children and deserted the family home – and I'm supposed to sign my name to it!'

'Don't mind what it says,' he said. 'Just sign, and then forget about it.'

'But I do mind,' she said. 'It isn't true! I didn't do anything wilfully and maliciously and I'm not going to sign that I did!'

The lawyer looked at her with concern. For him words were of no great account, it was the result which mattered. 'Look,' he said, 'it's just legal stuff.'

'I'll cross out the words "wilfully" and "maliciously",' she said, 'and then I'll sign it.'

'No,' he said, staying the pen with his hand, 'Don't! Listen to me, and believe me – it's a simple deal, Lilian. That's all it is, He needs you to be in the wrong, for his career – an officer is supposed to be a gentleman . . .'

'That's rich!' she interjected.

'. . . and it's bad for him to be divorced at all, but if he is the guilty party it's even more serious for him. He can be overlooked in the case of promotion, all that sort of thing. It's obviously important to him. Now, if you agree to be in the wrong – and never mind the words they use – you get the custody of the children, forever. Isn't it worth playing ball with him for that?'

Playing ball for your children! But everyone has his price. She signed it and then sat down suddenly, momentarily overcome.

He closed up his office then. 'Come on,' he said. 'I'm going to take you for a drink. I can't see you go like that! You'll feel better soon, now that it's all over.'

Those words again – it's all over. 'I know,' she said, 'I'm glad, really I am. It's a relief.'

Even though they were divorced now he would turn up unexpectedly, just phone from the airport to inform her he was on his way. The children, believing him home on leave from his ship, wherever it might be, would be overjoyed, so each time Lilian was obliged to conceal the stress she invariably felt, and treat the event as something to be celebrated.

After the routine of bedtime stories and childish

confidences, which he joined in to their delight, he would stand around while she did her evening chores, or sit on a kitchen stool. Once, as if unable to contain himself, he burst out, 'Look at you! You're thirty now, and what have you got to show for it?'

Without looking up from the ironing she had replied, 'I've got the children, that's enough for me.'

'The trouble with you,' he persisted, 'is that you have got no ambition.'

'No, I can't say I have. So what?'

'You've never known how to take advantage of your assets.'

'My assets?'

'Even when I met you, you were working in refugee camps – you could have been a *Vogue* model or a top sec-retary, or something like that.'

How, she thought, had they ever managed to get them-selves so mismatched? 'Look,' she said, 'this is a non-con-versation as far as I'm concerned. You do your thing, I'll do mine!'

At other times he seemed keen to talk about his own bizarre world; not his work, but peripheral matters, such as, for example, what he would do if he ever got wind of any suspicion concerning himself. His escape route was already planned, he told her; at any time he could dis-appear, have plastic surgery and re-emerge as someone else. She wasn't to be surprised, he said, if she was approached one day by someone who did not resemble him in the least, but had his voice.

[132]

Did he say these things to torture her? In the future she was to nearly get sick every time she recalled his words; the grotesque image of some man coming towards her with that unmistakable walk, the rolling gait of a sailor, and an unfamiliar face, and then to open his mouth and speak in that voice . . .

No, it probably didn't occur to him how repellent this information was to her; he might even have thought it quite funny himself, quite amusing – he had that sort of humour. More likely she thought, he merely needed to have someone listen to him; who else, after all, could he speak to of such things?

It also appeared he needed a dumping ground to unload his freakish gadgets; an expensive-looking leather case with a false bottom, an elaborate set of gold cuff links with long wires attached, for going up through the sleeves to a battery, miniscule tape recorders. 'I don't want them here,' she objected. 'Why can't you put them in a rubbish bin? Or burn them! Go and throw them in the sea! This is *my* home, I don't want those things in it!'

If only she could be left in peace! Would she ever feel free? Officially, of course, she was free, according to her divorce papers, but when you have been told, as she was, that a file is being kept on you, that your every movement is recorded, that the name and particulars of each friend, and new friend you make, is written down by some person who must be stalking you in order to compile this informa- tion, you don't feel exactly free. At first she had not believed him. 'Rubbish,' she had said. 'It couldn't be

[133]

someone's job just to follow me around, sticking his nose into my life. How boring he must find it, trailing me to school with the children, or round a supermarket! What a highlight it must be to watch me play a game of tennis – what a thrill! Sorry, but I don't believe it. I think you say these things just to make me feel I'm under your control. Why can't you leave me alone?'

'It's policy,' he had replied. 'You'd better believe it. I could look up any date and tell you what you were doing – in detail. I could tell you the number plate of any car you have been in.'

And it doesn't take much imagination to have an idea of the guilt Lilian felt, regarding her newly-made friends – neighbours, young couples, parents like herself with school-going children – who so readily proffered their friendship, little knowing that, by doing so, their names were being entered into files. Sometimes she felt she should withdraw completely, like a leper, live without friends, even acquaintances, but how? It was impossible – and with children, doubly impossible. So she carried on with her life in a more or less normal fashion, but with constant disquiet at the back of her mind, fearful of bringing harm to such decent and kind people; and saddened too, by the sense of loss, of deprivation, the realisation that she was denied the kind of deep friendships which evolve from shared confidences. Always she felt apart.

Time and again it seemed to her that as soon as she had got used to one situation, learned to cope with it and was actually managing to go along well again, another – new and worse – would present itself. Thankfully, Carl's visits were well spaced apart. Each time he came, she noticed new differences; he was growing into a stranger, his face, his whole appearance altering. Only rarely now would she catch an expression she recognised. But even despite this, until now there had persisted in her the conviction that he had not wholly ceased to care about her and the children. Some feeling did surely still exist, although it was not always in evidence, by any means.

'I want you to understand that it is out of the question for you to live in America.' This was his latest rant. 'I instructed my lawyer to put it in the divorce settlement, but he said he was unable to. So I have to tell you myself.'

'Well,' she said, 'it has never occurred to me to live in America. But if I wanted to, I would. Why not? It's not much further for you to visit the children.'

'I'm telling you not to.'

'And I'm telling you that I'm free to live where I want.'

'I'm afraid if you take that attitude, you won't last very long.'

'What exactly do you mean by that?'

'I mean that I wouldn't advise that attitude.'

'But what did you mean, I "wouldn't last very long"?'

'In plain language, if you do something you are told not to, you will be wiped out.'

'What!' She looked at his face, examining his expression. His eyes had a flat look about them. 'Wiped out! Do you mean bumped off?' Ridiculous euphemisms – he was talking about having her killed, murdered!

'That's the way it is,' he said. 'You'd better get used to it.'

'Oh, come on!' she said then, trying to keep the conversation on a normal level, to joke even. 'Ireland is a civilised country you know. You can't do that sort of thing here. They'd be on to you in no time, and you'd spend the rest of your life in prison!'

'It wouldn't be me.' He was quite serious. 'There are people to do these things.'

'I'm sorry, but you can't just murder people in Ireland when you feel like it. They are strict on that sort of thing here, it's not like South Africa!'

'It wouldn't be seen as murder. You would commit suicide.'

'I certainly would not! Leave the children uncared for!'

'You don't understand,' he said, as if they were discussing a mathematical problem. 'Look, you remember Robert McDaid? Well, he didn't commit suicide either! Got it now?'

'Robert McDaid didn't commit suicide! You mean he was murdered? But the letter from his sister . . .'

'He stepped out of line. And you had better bear in mind that the same could happen to you!'

'Why Robert McDaid? Was he a spy too?' She paused, and then said angrily, 'That's terrible! Don't you care? He was your friend – or perhaps he wasn't after all. Perhaps that was all a pretence. What sort of people are you mixed up with, for God's sake?'

There was no response in his face. 'The same thing,' he said, with heavy meaning in his voice, 'could happen to you, Lilian.'

'Don't talk nonsense!' she said. It was the only thing she could think of to say. She felt she was trying desperately to get the conversation out of cloud cuckoo land, back to the world as she knew it. 'Anyhow, I don't know what we are arguing about. I told you: it has never entered my head to live in America. It would be too far away from my father.'

He was mollified by that. It was true, she would not live that far from her father. But not satisfied that she fully real-ised the precariousness of her position, he laboured the point further – and she listened, humouring him to keep him from one of those devastating mood swings, but refusing at the same time to show she took him seriously.

After he had gone, left Ireland, bound for God knows where before going back to South Africa, she thought long about what he had said to her. And she tried to remember all the good things she could about him. Years ago he had wept when she had been seriously ill – was it really the same man who could look at her now with dead eyes, and make such utterances?

And yet, before he left, he had gone into still further detail of what might happen to her. Suicide, he had said, was not the only option. An accident could be arranged; a sudden jostle in a crowd, a well-aimed but discreet push at the right moment to send her off a pavement, or off the platform of a railway station or metro. There were many

[137]

methods open to experts, which would never be detected, never even be questioned by the authorities.

The point was, were these more lies of his? Or a true picture of her situation – a warning? One could not rule anything out, one way or the other. But he had not been lying about Robert McDaid, of that she felt sure. For, on reflection, he probably had been a spy himself, all that about his being depressed over his divorce just lies to give an excuse for his late night phone calls to Carl, and very likely they had known each other before they 'met' on the ship.

What sort of people were these who so totally disregarded all laws, made their own, and without the slightest qualms, disrupted the lives of all who came near them, or even accidentally crossed their paths? She remembered Carl speeding, in the black Alfa Romeo, ignoring the speed limit signs and how, when she had pointed out that he was breaking the law, he had replied, 'Laws are for fools!'

And what on earth had attracted Carl into this underworld of arrogance, betrayal and violence? Not, she was convinced, some intrinsic instinct, the way certain insects are drawn to slime and filth. Maybe he had even believed there was something heroic in what he had chosen to do with his life. Was he really, ideologically, a Communist? With his expensive tastes? Or was it, as he once said, that in his view, international espionage kept a necessary balance, prevented world domination by one power; that it provided a safety valve, for by learning each other's military secrets and plans, no one nation could rise to become too powerful. He had added that it was just a job, like any other.

Be that as it may, one of the universal canons of life seems to be that what we do, so we become – and Carl was now very much what his choice of work had made him. She felt intuitively that her way must be not to show she realised the danger she was in, not to accept it, not to allow it to affect their lives. Obviously confrontation would be foolhardy, best simply to behave in a rational common sense way, keeping life as normal as possible for the children.

Each time he came and went, there would follow for Lilian a period where everything he had said seemed to circulate restlessly in her consciousness, rather like the snow in those glass balls which children shake up into a storm and then wait for the flakes to settle. Mostly her snowflakes settled, too, but the fact that she might be murdered could not be ignored or rejected; the possibility was there, self evident, for how did 'they' know that she would not talk? How was it 'they' had let her live so long already, knowing what she knew? Any day one of those satanic men, 'experts' in getting rid of people, might appear in a crowd and push her under a bus. And who then would look after her children, love them, care for them as she did? These thoughts woke her often in the small hours and she would lie in a stupor of misery, imagining her children lost and bereft of all human warmth and decency, caught up in the insane world of their father's treachery, where people are 'wiped out' if they happened to be inconvenient.

But worse even, was the prospect of a contrived 'suicide', for then they would grow up believing she had chosen to leave them alone in the world; they would think she hadn't loved them enough to live for them. Who could help her? Whom could she trust, who would, in the eventuality, explain to her children that their mother had not killed herself; would never desert them; that there had been a mistake, but they must wait until they were older and could understand – but that they should always be sure of how much she had loved them?

But who? To whom could she say, 'Look, I may be murdered and if I am, I want you to do something for me.'? If their grandfather had been a younger man, his memory intact, there would be no question as to whom that person should be. She thought then of another member of the family. It would need to be someone who would continue to be in contact with the children as they grew up.

She tried, when she was next in England, but failed. He was reproving, 'I don't think you should say things like that!' Hands clammy, painful constrictions in her chest, breathless, she was unable to continue. She knew she should behave normally, overrule him, say: I'm sorry, but you have got to listen to me! But she couldn't do it, something powerful was threatening to overwhelm her, she felt she would be ill if she tried again.

Her second attempt was with a family friend of long standing, a very decent man (and being a doctor he would have sworn the Hippocratic oath, be capable of secrecy) but she failed with him too. He laughed heartily at her and told her not to fantasise, teasing her: did she think she was making herself more interesting? Once more the same occurrence of sweating palms, breathlessness, constrictions in the chest. She felt her whole body trembling and had the sensation of being on the brink of something unfamiliar and frightening. Fearing hysteria, she was relieved when he changed the subject and started talking about something quite different and again she felt unable to persevere.

The realisation that she was not as strong as she would like to be, or thought she should be, depressed her and gave a negative turn to her spirits. With no access to justice, no security, no redress; deprived of normal commonplace human rights, she felt disconnected, severed like a leaf in the wind, from the general community. How could she make a good life for her children? If they picked up her feelings of inadequacy and depression at this stage of their young lives, it could mar their future attitudes; they might become negative too, ineffective and crabbed in outlook.

The catalyst came in the form of a letter from her father, with a cheque. He knew she was owed some money, which was not forthcoming, and had decided to intervene. 'Buy a car,' he told her, 'get yourself and the children out and around. It can't be doing you any good, cooped up in a small flat, with no transport.'

Yes, she thought, that's it, of course! That's it! We don't know what might happen, but by God we are going to enjoy ourselves for as long as we can!

It was summer then, and she bought a second-hand Triumph Herald with a canvas roof; it seemed more like a boat on wheels with the hood down, and the children loved piling in with buckets and spades, towels and picnic baskets, and driving off over the mountains, down to the miles of white sandy beaches strung along the coasts of Counties Wicklow and Wexford. The more outings they did, and the more of the surrounding countryside they explored, the more inventive they became. They would take paints and paper and lie on river banks or under mountain larch trees, painting wild flowers and leaves or whatever took their fancy. They lit fires, cooked food and boiled water for their teas. The changing seasons brought no diminishment of their outdoor pleasures; every Saturday and Sunday they would still drive off to enjoy themselves, regardless of weather. And it was fun to take flasks of soup, and to cook sausages and potatoes in their jackets, sheltered by trees or by grassy cliffs, from the misty rains and winds. When it snowed, they would put chains on the car wheels and take their toboggans up into the mountains, to fly down the hills, shouting and laughing and startling the wild deer.

Sometimes they would go for joint picnics with other families from the square; three or four carloads, meeting at some arranged point in the mountains, or on one of the long more or less deserted beaches; spending whole days walking, swimming, lazing and sharing their food.

Convinced she was on the right track – for the children were clearly blooming (herself, too, unhealthy anxieties pushed to one side, almost forgotten), she felt she was entering a new period of her life. By now, entirely at home in Ireland, she had friends such as she had longed for and been denied in South Africa; people who, while widely varying in character and background, had at core interests and values similar to her own. And though alone now, a single parent, there was always someone, or several, enquiring if she would like to go with them to the cinema or for a game of tennis, or to bring the children to play, and she was glad and grateful to join in the life of the community.

Through these friends, she gradually met friends of theirs, too, from other parts of Dublin, and soon after that any morning she might happen to walk down Grafton Street, in the city centre, she would be quite likely to meet someone or other she knew, who might suggest a walk through St Stephen's Green park, or a coffee in Bewley's Cafe, or a chat in a pub over a glass of Guinness. It was one such morning, heavily overcast, threatening thunder, that she was persuaded to go to a fortune-teller with two friends she met on the pavement, a few yards from Bewley's, where she was about to take refuge. It was just starting to spatter large drops of rain. 'Come on,' they urged, 'it will cheer us all up. She's great fun!'

She was a diminutive old lady, with scanty white hair and only two teeth, the front ones, so that her appearance was strikingly that of a little white rabbit. Her room was cosy, with a fire (also diminutive) in the grate, and she smiled in such a friendly and delightful way that Lilian, going in for her turn, somewhat sceptical, was immediately charmed. Moments later, she sat electrified as the woman told her that she had been married to a man involved in espionage, working for the Russians, and that if she had stayed abroad, she would no longer be alive. She then described how Lilian had been a motherless child, reared by her father, and finally dismissing her, added with a chuckle that she had done very well to get herself divorced from the spy. 'Ireland is good for you!' was her parting remark.

And so it seemed to be. Life on the whole was good, a variety of aspects opening up for her. In particular, she was aware of a new kind of confidence, something entirely removed from her previous self-assurance, which had merely been the consequence of an easy lifestyle, no thanks to personal qualities. Hitherto, simply by writing a cheque, not even seeing the money, her wishes had been fulfilled, leaving her with a pleasant sensation of gratification and control. Now she had learned (and would never again imagine to the contrary) just how far she was from being in control, and somehow this had liberated her, for she had ceased to worry about security; she had faced and accepted the fact that, for her anyway, there was no such thing and, in doing so, freed herself from the desire for it. For what was the point of desiring something which did not exist? No longer seeing herself as master or mover of her fate, she had come to feel there was some far greater thing, whatever name you wanted to put on it, which she somehow had to be open to, go along with rather than fight against, and be guided by; which she must trust in, and believe (despite appearances) that 'all manner of things shall be well'. Instead of imagining herself in control, she saw herself as sailing her boat on the high seas of life, dealing as best she could with the vagaries of storm and calm alike – each situation as it arose – and it seemed to her that everyone else, without exception, was doing the same. And from this she felt for the first time kinship with fellow beings, people known and unknown, for one tempest is after all much like another, apart from a few unimportant details, and the difference between a squall and a gale only a matter of degrees.

Recalling her years of isolation in South Africa, it occurred to her that much of her loneliness had in fact been self-induced, in that she had excluded herself from the company of those whose views she disapproved of; and she wondered now if there wasn't, in the state of isolation, a danger of becoming self-righteous. Better perhaps, if she had seen in each person a vulnerable human being. But to do that, she would have had to be aware of her own vulnerability; and there, protected, cushioned by the comforts of a beautiful home and high living standards, she had not yet discovered it.

Yes, the fortune-teller had been right: Ireland was good for her. She still had bouts of anxiety, still dreaded sudden phone calls from the airport, or that she might have to see Carl unrecognisably altered by plastic surgery; still worried that she might herself bring harm, through her connection with him, to her family or friends, and most of all, of course, she feared the sudden appearance of unknown men in her home – that her children might be left alone in the world without her love. But all this was now contained in a separate compartment of her mind, and seemed to have nothing to do with the new freedom and enjoyment of family life, both in Dublin and during the school holidays in Devonshire.

So while on the one hand everything seemed to be going along well, or well enough, on the other there was an irony in having to be grateful that she was still alive; that she had not been murdered, at least up until now.

9

Imperceptibly the years rolled around, like great unseen wheels, the spokes the rotating succession of birthdays, Christmases, Easters, Hallo'eens, turning from season to season. And with them, the pattern of school terms and holidays, with the usual quota of concerts, plays, sports events; the expeditions to buy books, uniforms, equipment of all sorts; the inevitable bouts of measles, mumps, chicken pox and the odd, mercifully few, accidents of broken limbs, cuts to be stitched, all intermingled with the successes and failures, sorrows and joys, highs and lows that every family experiences to a greater or lesser degree.

In the centre of everything, the hub, was the created illusion of normality, for Lilian was determined above all on normality, regardless of what might or might not happen in the future. Of course she herself would never again feel wholly normal, she knew that a corner of her self would have to remain covert, restricted, but nevertheless she found that by living life as if it were normal, it became normal; that it was possible for the most part to make your life what you wanted. And if your nature was to be happy, you could still be so. It was a matter of attitude, of whether or not you could say to hell with the sword of Damocles poised over your head, and live as if it simply wasn't there.

Now it was only rarely that she thought about the dreaded strangers, the sub-species of men who might be sent by the KGB to disrupt her family, to annihilate her. Instead it was their absence that she pondered on. Had Carl lied to his bosses; told them she knew nothing, that he had not after all attempted to recruit her, believing her unsuitable material? Or said that their marriage had broken down for other reasons, and he had therefore refrained from broaching the subject? And had they believed him?

It seemed at any rate a possible explanation for being left, however temporarily, to get on with her life.

But if this were so, what would be his reasons, his motives, for lying about her? Had he a conscience? Or (and was this perhaps more likely) was she of more use to him alive than dead? For it occurred to her that, as a South African with no connections overseas, ostensibly a naval officer whose only base was the Simonstown dockyard in Capetown, he was obviously in need of a legitimate reason for his many trips to Europe where, according to him, he ran a spy ring. What better cover than to be known as a conscientious father keeping in touch with his children –

never mind if in truth Ireland was but rarely included in his travels.

Another important consideration must have been the question of how he would cope with having to look after the children himself, should the mother be 'wiped out' as he chose to put it. Presumably it would rather clip the wings of a high-flying spy to suddenly find himself responsible for a family and, aware as he was of his limitations as a father, he must have decided it was to his advantage to leave things be.

It would be interesting to know what made Carl so certain that Lilian would not betray him by reporting him to the authorities; and equally it might be wondered whether – in view of the danger she was in – this had not in fact been contemplated by her. In the case of Carl, probably it was nothing more than that extraordinary, not to say arrogant, confidence in his own judgement, pre-requisite of a spy if he is to last; while the answer concerning Lilian lay in the customary penalties for high treason. That she might send anyone, let alone the father of her children, to the gallows or in front of a firing squad, was unthinkable. It would be unliveable with. If it had been merely a question of prison, she would perhaps have considered the matter in a different light, but this she was not to know for the situation existed as it was, immutable, there was nothing she could do about it.

Looking for part time work that would fit in with school and playschool hours was discouraging, not to say depressing, for it seemed to be the province of rogues, out to exploit the single mother who would gratefully accept low wages, and raise no objection to the waiving of tax and welfare stamps in return for hours that suited the needs of small children. Lilian soon found it was that or nothing and, like all the others in the same position, learned to put up with it cheerfully, doing each job for as long as it could be tolerated – which sometimes was only for a short while. Like, for example, the furniture removal firm round the corner from where she lived, who employed her to sit in their office and answer telephone calls. She had imagined this was for the purpose of making bookings and so on, but in fact it was to be a go-between, a buffer, between the boss and his outraged clients, who rang constantly to complain of broken and destroyed items of every sort, and to demand compensation. Some of them told Lilian they had been trying to contact the man, either by post or telephone, for over a year.

'Tell them I'm down in the country on a job,' 'Tell them I'm abroad.' 'Tell them I've gone to a funeral.' 'Tell them anything, just make it up!' He was incorrigible, he couldn't care less.

'I can't be a paid liar,' she told him, but he just laughed, he thought she was joking.

'You'll get used to it,' he'd said, not seeing it was that she was afraid of.

And indeed, but for that fear she might well, in the name of expediency – for the job was so conveniently near her home, the hours so suitable for the children – have stayed on, persuading herself that the responsibility for the lies was his, not hers.

Then she worked for two elderly solicitors down on the quays. Their place, overlooking the River Liffey, was old and dusty, delightful, Dickensian; they seemed to be completely behind the times and Lilian never saw a client the whole time she was there, only friends passing in and out for a chat. She couldn't see how they made any money but they assured her that clients came in the afternoons, when she had gone. There was some typing now and then for her to do, on an old manual machine, but as mostly they expected her to type from a dictaphone that didn't work properly, and worse, when it did, she couldn't make out what they said because they both had strong Cork accents, one way or another, very little seemed to be accomplished by anyone. The crunch came when they couldn't pay her and hopefully suggested reducing her already low wages, and she had to explain that the reason she worked was because she needed the money. She parted from them quite sorrowfully because she had become fond of them and their little dusty room, with their cronies dropping in, but clearly it was some kind of a scam, tax evasion or something of the sort.

She thought at last she had landed herself something good when she replied to an advertisement in the *Irish Times* to cook a 'high class' lunch every day for a business firm in St Stephen's Green. She went for an interview and duly got a letter saying that she had been chosen. Two weeks later, half dead from exhaustion, practically speechless, she handed in her resignation. Each day had started with the shopping, which entailed going to the best shops in Dublin for fresh salmon here, steak there, vegetables somewhere else, and so on. All this then had to be lugged up the back stairs of the imposing building, to the top floor where they had made a specially designed and rather pretentious dining room with a small kitchen off. There Lilian had to prepare and cook a three-course meal for between fifteen to twenty businessmen – it varied from day to day and sometimes at short notice they invited guests. This she would do frantically and at top speed, with not even one extra pair of hands to help peel potatoes or anything, trying to beat the clock and be ready to lay the table for the appointed time. Then, unbelievably, she would be expected to change into good clothes, mingle with the diners, pour wine, serve each course and carry out the dirty dishes, returning finally with freshly made coffee. After they had left, she would change back into her working clothes, do all the washing up, clean the kitchen and on the way out she was charged to take the day's table-cloth and napkins to a laundry shop. This was supposed to be a part-time job, and for it she was paid twelve pounds a week, a pittance even then. No, she said to herself, I'd rather live on bread and water.

By now Carl had a spy-partner wife – Swiss-German, pro-duced, according to him, by the Russians as suitable, already on their payroll. Contact with his children had less-ened steadily over the years, his visits to Ireland infrequent

– although after one extraordinary incident, she could not even be sure of that.

The fact that Lilian's boss at this particular time – a catalogue publisher in the city centre – was South African, had made no impression on her when she was interviewed for the job. Relieved, on hearing the familiar accent, that she had used her maiden name, Prowse, in her application, she had adopted her customary silence concerning her own association with the country, knowing that if she mentioned she had lived there, the questions would begin: Really! Whereabouts? Ah, that's near Simonstown, isn't it? Where the navy is? Were you connected to the navy, then? What was your husband's name? I might know him . . . and so on. Like a chess player anticipating the moves ahead, she had learned that to avoid being forced into a difficult position, the best strategy was to skirt the subject.

A pleasant enough man, he seemed to like coming into her small office where she had to type endless lists on an unfamiliar type of computer machine which (since she was by no means gifted in this field) she only barely had the hang of. She wasn't sure whether his purpose was to check she wasn't slacking, or because he felt like some conversation – or both. He appeared to enjoy talking rather boastfully about himself, his large house in Killiney (a very expensive area, he assured her, as if it wasn't common knowledge) and his connections with South Africa. He also appeared to have an almost pathological anxiety that he should have good relations with his employees, and would question her as to the morale of the girls in the paste-up room. They, of

course, were all well aware of this and used to laugh about
it when they met for breaks in the little kitchenette, telling
Lilian they were convinced he had their workroom bugged;
that whenever they talked about difficulties in their work as
they sat doing paste-ups around the large table, he would
miraculously appear and start to discuss the same thing,
as if by chance, giving his own opinion and directions.
And when they complained about the cheap brand of
instant coffee he provided, that same day there was a fresh,
untouched jar of Nescafe in the kitchenette. They found it
all quite hilarious and regaled Lilian and one another with
each new instance, each new proof that he listened in on
them. Lilian did not know quite what to make of it, thinking that maybe it was simply a game of invention, to make
life more interesting, to spice it up a bit, until one afternoon
when he was chatting in her office, he suddenly remarked,
again in that slightly boastful manner, as if he wanted to
shock her, or impress her, 'I don't make any money from
this business you know – not a penny!'

'Really?' she said. 'How do you make your living then?'

'Aha,' he replied, 'I get money sent from South Africa.'

'Oh, I see,' she said, as if it were perfectly normal to
come to Ireland, buy a business, employ people, work at it
every day, and not be concerned about making money
from it because your funding came from another source in
another country. 'You just do it for fun, do you?'

At that he merely smiled a superior smile, as if to say:
'That's given you something to think about!' and removed
himself.

A couple of months later, Carl made an appearance in Dublin – a visit to see the children, he said – and they all had lunch in the Shelbourne Hotel. At a certain point, Lilian said, 'I'm working for a South African now. He publishes catalogues.'

Carl's face went blank and she knew that meant he was alert. Watching him, she added, 'I don't know why he bothers, he told me he makes no profit from the business, and that all his money comes from South Africa.'

His face stayed motionless, not a muscle moved, and then he said, as if to himself, 'He did, did he?' And she guessed then that she had somehow managed to get herself mixed up in his world again.

It was a Sunday, and as he sat drinking coffee and smoking a cigar, the children questioned him, 'How long are you going to be in Ireland?' 'When are you leaving?'

'Tuesday,' he told them.

'Shall we get permission to be off school tomorrow?'

'No, I have a very important meeting tomorrow.'

'Next day then?'

'No, I won't have time to see you again.'

When Lilian arrived at work the next morning, pulling her bicycle in at the elegant Georgian front door, she was greeted by the girls. 'The boss won't be in all day – he's got a very important meeting.'

He had not come in the following day either. When she next met him the smiles and heartiness were gone, replaced by an immaculately friendly and polite manner; cold eyes that seemed to rest speculatively upon her when he thought she wasn't looking. Or was she imagining it?

And did she imagine the relief on his face when she gave in her notice at the end of the week? Had his regret been feigned or genuine? The truth was, of course, that she simply didn't know, couldn't know, and would never know. She didn't even want to know. What she did want, more than anything, was to be free of Carl, free of his world; free of imaginings, of suspicions, of spectres – to be free, free, free. She didn't want to go on having to meet him, to be obliged to listen to his views, to have to sift, or try to sift, truth from lies, sense from delusions. She didn't want to hear stories such as how he was jumped on in a dark alleyway by five men, all of whom he left for dead or unconscious. Why did he tell her these things? He knew it would not impress her, rather that she would be disgusted. It was more as though he wanted this, to disgust her, and at the same time to force her to see through his eyes; to say to her: 'Look, your simplistic little world doesn't really exist! It's make-believe land! Grow up! Stop being so naïve! My world is the real world!' She felt he hated and scorned everything she valued; her beliefs, her aspirations; that he somehow wanted to crush them out of her.

Yes, freedom would be good all right, but with her children as hostages to fortune, she had to settle for the fact that it was out of her reach, not on the cards; the best she could do was to put on the usual front of normality and make sure that such meetings with Carl passed as pleasantly as possible for all concerned. For much as she dreaded them, they were still vastly preferable to his taking the children out of the country, on holiday, which was the alternative, and which, on rare occasions, he did. This he was entitled to do of course, by law, it was in the divorce paper, and even if it were not, any attempt at refusal would for certain precipitate a kidnapping, perhaps on a permanent basis. He always made sure she understood the mafia-type power and control at his disposal – it didn't bear thinking of.

She would never forget the first time he took them away from her, for a week to London. Still barely more than babies, she had felt she was being cut with a knife as she watched them leave, her only consolation that they had gone off trustingly serious, excited to be with their father.

Another time, just days before Christmas, he had sent his spy wife to fetch them and escort them to South Africa. All the past week they had been decorating the rooms with holly, and the tall tree looked beautiful with white wax candles, the way they always did it each year. To have her children taken out of her home by a woman who was a spy, by definition with opposite values and principles to her own; to see them leave, crying and unwilling, was more, Lillian felt, than should be asked of anyone. No one but herself could know the extent of her pain.

As they grew older, there were skiing holidays, Davos, St Moritz, and it was exciting for them to fly over to Geneva on their own, to be met and taken shopping for the various paraphernalia of ski clothes, ice skates, with expensive presents thrown in, and then make their ascent by train high up into the snowy mountains, through forests, along the edge of sheer gorges, until they reached the resort and all the buzz that went with it.

To the children, and to the outside world in general, it was their right to spend time with their father, and they assured Lilian it was good fun, at least for the most part. As always, there were the tensions they had learned to associate with him, but these they weathered with the cheerful philosophy of children bent on enjoying themselves, caught up as they were in the daily activities of their respective ski classes.

For Lilian, the effort of giving the impression to her father, her friends, and to the children themselves, that all was as it should be was immense, for it was untrue, it was not what she felt. Had she been convinced Carl really cared about his children and wanted time to be with them, to get to know them, to establish a loving parental relationship with them, then despite everything, she would have been genuinely glad, but the fact was she distrusted his motives. Was he using the children to present a picture of an innocent family holiday, while carrying on his work, having contact with other criminal characters? The thought that her children might be being used to further his ends was repugnant, a profanity, and gave rise to a feeling of fury against him. How dare he contaminate them with his world?

They would come back into the grey Irish winter – golden tans, shining eyes, sun-streaked hair – their talk all of snow, hot chocolate, other children they had made friends with. There were bruises to be shown, acquired from tumbles on the ice rink or on the slopes; funny stories to be told, re-lived, laughed over.

One story, less funny than the others, was that the oldest, up late, had overheard her father and his spy-partner wife discussing whether to put an end to Lilian's life, have her got rid of. Pandemonium had broken out, hysteria all round, followed by persuasion that it was only a joke.

'Wasn't it funny, Mummy?' She saw guilt in their faces at having been coerced into laughing at something they knew was in bad taste, but anxiety, too, not wanting to see something wrong with their father.

'Well, I expect you didn't like it very much, really?'

'No, we didn't.' Relief that it was now out in the open, relief that she understood.

'Don't mind it,' she said. 'He meant it to be funny, like a spooky story – you know, like you get at Hallowe'en parties. That kind of thing. You like them, don't you?'

'Yes . . . sort of.'

'People are all different, you have to remember that. Everyone has a different idea of what's funny; a different sense of humour.'

And in the way children have of wanting to be sure, to

be clear in their minds, they were looking at her earnestly, 'So . . . so it was "sort-of" funny?'

'Yes,' she said, '"sort-of".'

'Dad's "sort-of"?'

'That's right. His "sort-of" funny.'

10

To some extent, until she had left South Africa, she had always been at least relatively dependent, first on her father, then on Carl. Ireland for her, then, was a place of personal growth, of making advances and making mistakes, probably in even proportion; but all in all, generally speaking, she never had cause to disagree with the old woman, the fortune-teller, who had said that Ireland was good for her. Not a country that hits you immediately with obvious statements, like tropical beaches or deserts and pyramids, she felt instead the land and people opening up to her little by little, surely and unhurriedly; a two-way arrangement, the more she put in of herself, the more glimpses were exposed to her of something barely palpable – of a misty quality, like the mountains with their low clouds, ever-changing greens and dark peat-stained streams – but nevertheless powerful enough to bind her into a relationship for life.

Of Carl, at this time, she would hear more than she would see. Forgetting his existence for the most part, she would be forced back reluctantly into a state of remembering by strange stories – such as that he had turned up unexpectedly at her father's house in Devon, and requested the loan of a car. Her father, who treated everyone with courtesy, and certainly knew no reason not to do so concerning the father of his grandchildren, had been glad enough to help him out, whatever it was he needed to do – but somewhat surprised days later when the car was returned with thousands of miles clocked up, and positively no explanation offered: just 'thanks' and he was gone.

Lilian's father was rather amused by this episode and, having a lively imagination, started telling everyone he knew that he thought his ex-son-in-law was really a sort of James Bond. For quite some years he enjoyed his invention and resisted the cold water Lilian tried to pour on it. This in turn was not helped by the fact that when she and the children were next in Devon with him, and the children also heard his theory, they, too, thought the idea hilarious and chimed in with their own observations of how the last time they had seen their father, he had taken to wearing long coats with fur collars and the sort of black leather gloves worn by criminals in films. From then on they had continued to laugh about 'Dad's spy outfits', and were half-convinced he dressed up on purpose to try and look like a spy. Lilian would inwardly roll her eyes up to heaven and wonder how much more insane the situation could become.

Gradually, after that, everything she heard from Carl's quarter seemed to indicate a growing state of megalomania, or some kind of power complex. By now she wanted nothing more to do with him, but for his part it appeared as though he couldn't, or wasn't prepared to, let go of her completely, was determined to keep some sort of control over her. He would write letters, almost unbelievable in content. For example once it was an order that if the children didn't do well at school in their exams, she, Lilian, was to beat them, and if she didn't comply with his instructions, he would fly over from South Africa and do it himself personally.

She felt one could only ignore such ravings, so she started to throw his letters away unopened – why should they spoil her day? – and ceased altogether to reply. His next move was to arrange with a lawyer, the same one that had dealt with the divorce papers, that he would in future send his letters to him, and that he, the lawyer, was to read them out to Lilian. This way he would know that Lilian had heard every word he wanted to say, every command he wanted to make, every notion he wanted to impress on her.

She had agreed, to avoid a worse situation, and although between them they never discussed Carl, she knew well what the lawyer thought of him. Sometimes, to cheer her up and make her laugh, he would joke on the phone, 'I've had another letter from Goebbels, could you come in to the office?'

So she would drive into Dublin and sit in a big leather

armchair while he read out the latest list of orders and instructions. Then, without any reference to it, the lawyer would tear it up, drop it into the wastepaper basket and simply ask her how she was, talk about something unconnected, and that would be that until the next time.

It could be considered harmless enough, from such a distance, but it galled her sorely. The nerve of him! She had all the responsibility for the welfare of the children in every sense: physical, moral, emotional, educational; their health, happiness and outlook depended entirely on the decisions she had to make. Who, then, was he to consider himself entitled to lay down his own laws, and half-baked ones at that?

And she was obliged to endure it, to listen to his lunatic rantings. She would sit, her face impassive, inscrutable, not a muscle moving, to hide her humiliation. What could this lawyer, this nice man, think of her that she didn't react, get to her feet, instruct him to tell Carl to go to hell, to get out of her life once and for all?

One time, looking at her closely, he said, 'If ever he gives you any trouble, you can be sure I will take your part in any court in the world, and I will see to it that he is made to leave you alone.'

She thanked him, moved, but heavy-hearted in the knowledge that normal avenues, as pursued by others, did not exist for her. How could she explain that Carl had pavement-pushers, exterminators, at his disposal; people who could arrange a suicide with less effort than it would take her to lay on a childrens tea party?

However, the events of the past years had taught her not to dwell on dark thoughts; she had developed the capacity to sever from her mind all circumstances that she could do nothing about. Within minutes of leaving the office, she would forget what had taken place, except the kindness of the lawyer; it was her way of refusing to allow Carl to intrude on her space, her territory, her currently pleasant existence.

Her father's death, the teenage years of her children, all passed by under what seemed an ever-changing and turbulent sky; periods of tranquillity could be turned over night to gales and tempests, times of fun and harmony be overtaken by indescribable pain. After her father died she knew, and she was right, that for her the world without him in it would never again be the same place. She dealt with the loss the only way she knew, the way her life of enforced secrecy and reticence had geared her – that is, not to speak about her feelings (which did not meant to stifle them, but to have them and deal with them alone) and to get on with other things.

A major concern at the time, as for all parents of teenagers, was the question of drugs, rampant, apparently, around Dublin. According to what her own children told her, from the age of twelve upwards, you could not walk through the city with a friend on a Saturday morning to spend your pocket money, without being approached and offered something or other. Lilian, reasonably confident, knew that to be over-confident would be foolhardy. The most dangerous times, it seemed, were the holidays, when the regular and trusted friends were away out of Dublin. Then, for a number of weeks, especially in the summer, in the dusty heat and long evenings, you could see bored and depressed-looking children hanging around the back streets, vandalising cars, looking for new chance acquaintances, other bored unfortunates with whom to alleviate the tedium and monotony of their lives.

Action struck her as the best preventative. Unable to afford hotel holidays, they equipped themselves with cheap tents and sleeping bags and headed south across Europe by train and boat to the Greek islands. In Corfu they asked a local farmer for permission to camp in an olive grove beside a small bay and, fires being hazardous at the time of year, promised to use the nearby taverna for meals, toilets and showers. Each day they would get up early and swim in the blue transparent sea before going for breakfast, and later in the day, as they lay reading in the shade of the trees, the farmer or his wife or children or relatives would pass by and bring them gifts of fruit from their orchards or vines.

One morning, Lilian stuck her head out of her tent before the children had awoken and saw, in the silence of one of those golden Greek mornings, the sea catching and reflecting the first rays of the sun, the entire olive grove filled with the flutterings wings of large blue butterflies. And as she watched them she thought of how her life had changed, and how if it hadn't, she might never have experienced the magical sight in front of her at that moment.

She thought, too, of the train journey down to Brindisi, how tired they had been, standing in the packed corridor, not even room to sit on their rucksacks; how well the children had endured it and not complained once. And she asked herself, almost in wonder, was that really me who used to travel first class in trains, with a hat box sometimes, or one of those long cardboard boxes with a balldress wrapped in tissue paper inside?

They had spent practically all the weeks of the summer holiday there in Corfu, having no wish to budge from the olive grove. They often spoke of how little one actually needed to be happy when in beautiful and congenial surroundings, and how many artificial needs were created to satisfy people who were bored.

Once more in Ireland, they continued to talk of their holiday, remembering all the details, the kindness of the farmer and his family, the meals in the taverna, swimming at night in the moonlight, the fireflies, and how they had watched the swallows at dusk, swooping low, skimming the smooth surfaces of the ground, and each making a huge effort, it seemed, to outdo the performance of the last.

And as term started and the leaves on the trees turned colour and began to drop, there was a feeling among them all of fulfilment and satisfaction, of a summer well spent. They say the child is father to the man – is that what it meant, she wondered, the way she was learning so much that she hadn't known before, alongside her children?

There were things, too, that she was trying to teach them, warn them in their early years, in advance, such as how when you have taken the wrong road, a path not in keeping with your true self, probably the most important thing in your life is to be able to turn back each time, change your mind, get on the right road again – things she herself was only now, during these years, discovering for herself.

The following spring, needing to change their car, instead of buying something practical as she had intended, Lilian allowed herself to be persuaded into getting an old ex-army Land Rover which rattled and banged and was neither comfortable nor economical, but was solid and, in fact, a great deal of fun. The children were growing up so fast, soon they wouldn't be with her any longer; plenty of time then for being sensible. With four-wheeled drive and eight gears, it was hardly the best car for learners to practise on, but up in the mountains, along the forest mud tracks, over logs and fallen branches, through streams and bogs and small ravines, it proved ideal for adventurous teenagers. They would picnic too; light fires, cook potatoes and sausages. Sometimes, near to a clearing where they would be sitting, some deer might pass noiselessly out from the trees, stare at them and then disappear into a clump of bracken and foxgloves, back into the forest.

At the same time, there were exams to be contended with, careers to think about; and, more and more, as her children neared adulthood, life in the outside world was beckoning them.

It seemed to Lilian that, before leaving home, her children had the right to know something (what, she was not quite sure) of their father's double life. Certainly not that he was a spy; nothing that could put them at risk or be a burden to them. Merely so that if anything should happen, it would not come as too much of a shock. She spent months thinking about it, and even after that waited until the point in each of their lives – separately, individually – where she felt they might be ready. When it seemed the appropriate moment, she said things in a matter-of-fact sort of way, without drama, like, 'Maybe you should know that I don't believe the work your father does is entirely what it appears to be.' In each case she found her remarks responded to with little or no real surprise, perhaps even a faint relief, and replies such as, 'It probably isn't.' 'You couldn't know with him.' 'You'd never know what he might be up to.' And she was led to wonder what they had seen or observed on holidays that she didn't know about. More likely though, it was simply that they felt he was a tricky sort of person.

Much later they were to tell her that they were very glad to have been given this slight hint or warning, or anyway to have had their own suspicions confirmed that all was not quite as he would have them believe; that it had, in fact, to a small extent at least, prepared them for the bombshell when it came.

In the meantime, these particular years combined into what seemed to Lilian almost a separate era entire unto itself. Third level education became the next issue; new friends, old school friends, more camping trips, student houses, then their own flats, partners, all falling into place one after the other. By now Lilian was working on the other side, the north side, of the city, as a childcare worker with battered children from violent homes.

Before starting the work, still at the interviewing stage, some said of her intention, 'You can't do that kind of work – you haven't the right appearance or voice. Working in the poorest parts of Dublin, you'd be anathema to the people who live there. They wouldn't trust you. They'd see you as an English do-gooder.'

What an indictment – discouraging to say the least. Was it possible she would be seen as an enemy in some way, just because of her voice? Why always these barriers between people? She remembered how disadvantaged she had felt by her colour, her language, her husband's position in South Africa; the false barriers that had existed between herself and Teena, and Caroline and Harry – the only people around her she had really liked.

I can't change my voice. Anyway, it's my father's voice, I learned to speak from him. Why should I be ashamed of it? I am who I am, and people will have to like or dislike me according to how they find me – not how I sound. And she wondered how many people, in how many varieties of situations, had said the same thing to themselves.

She went through all the arguments in her head, not

needing to convince herself, but thinking of those who might be prejudiced. In fact she needn't have given the matter a thought; it was good to learn that such considerations were non-existent.

She learned other things, too; that in family violence there were no boundaries of class or education (the only difference being that well-off victims were not dependent on the state for assistance and did not need to apply for refuge) and that in the very worst areas of poverty and deprivation, where drunkenness, violence and hopelessness were rife, there, where she least expected it, she came across probably more generosity, kindness, courage and plain decency than she had encountered anywhere previously, in any of the various other social spheres she had been accustomed to move in.

A long-time member of Amnesty International, Lilian found that between the two bus journeys to work (one from the south side into the city centre, the other to the north side) she was walking every day past the offices. One evening she went in. They were short-staffed. After that, two nights a week on her way home from work, she stopped in to help run the office and type letters.

And so it was that now, instead of doing just any old job that happened to fit in with term-time hours or which left her free for school holidays, she was selecting work that suited her, work she wanted to do for the sake of what it was; which was her choice, and which brought her colleagues with similar interests and outlook. With it there were new aspirations, new goals, the rewards of achievement. At work there had been early promotion, and at an Amnesty AGM, in recognition of time put in, she had found herself elected to the Board. In general, it was a good time for her.

It was eye-opening, too, a revelation, and she felt herself more and more drawn to the world outside her normal, or usual, horizons. And it was almost like a gift that these new interests came to her just at the time when all parents, and perhaps more so the single parent, are faced with the empty nest; proud and glad on the one hand to see their offspring succeeding to make their way, sad on the other to be no longer necessary to them.

Being responsible for home and children had never presented a problem to her, rather she had always considered it both pleasure and privilege, and had felt sorry during the 'sixties and 'seventies to hear women activists complaining about the burden of child-rearing and the drudgery of housework. Against all forms of inequality, whether concerning man, woman or child, she had nevertheless always seen childcare and home-making as an expression of love, not connected in any way to the concepts of justice or injustice.

Regarding her own situation, she had felt only that while her children were at home, her responsibility was to be 'around' – in the background, watchful and physically present. Any thoughts of going for a career, exerting full-time energies outside, she had put, without regrets, on a long arm. There would be time for that later. And now it had come.

Sometimes, in retrospect, she would wonder if she had done the right thing, in trying to foster some kind of small spark in the relationship between Carl and the children, when they were still very young – buying presents and cards from him at birthdays and Christmases; urging him to write to them. Perhaps it would have been better for them if she hadn't, but it's hard to know at the time. Now it was no longer anything to do with her whether they corresponded or not. It was their own private business. He would still make rare and unheralded appearances and, to Lilian, who would try to avoid him whenever possible, it seemed his aspect grew more sinister each time.

Indeed, there was no denying he looked his part. She hoped the children did not see him as she did, and was shocked then to learn that one of them had dreamt that for a twenty-first birthday present, their father had sent a letter-bomb through the post.

It had been a really good day. She had been given a batch of tickets for the cinema, and had taken a group of teenagers to see the film, *Gandhi*. Of course they hadn't wanted to go. 'Who would want to see a film about an *old* man? An *old, black* man! Why can't we see something else – there's lots of better films on.'

'Well,' she said, 'it's that or nothing. We've been given the tickets free – so it's take it or leave it.'

They had dragged their feet unwillingly into the cinema, complaining bitterly about everything, until the lights went off and they had to be quiet. But at the interval they had all leaned up to her from both sides of the row they were sitting in, their faces (usually sceptical, streetwise) rapt and impressed. 'It's great, isn't it?' 'He's a sort of black Jesus Christ, isn't he?'

She would often drop in on one or other of her own children on her way back from work. This time, looking forward to talking about the film, and the reaction of the teenagers, she knocked as usual and, since the door was open, went in. There was silence. Normally there would be laughter and friends around.

'What's wrong?' she said. 'What's the matter?'

'Dad's been arrested. It was on the radio. He was arrested in America by the FBI. They say he's a Russian spy. It's true, I suppose? That he's a spy?'

'Yes,' she said. 'I'm afraid it is.' And seeing in her mind a young man, an almost boy of twenty-one, laughing, as he had been when she had first known him, she put her hands to her face and wept; she wept for him, for her children, for herself, and for the senselessness of it all.

Part Three

———— ◆ ————

I I

When they had first gone out to South Africa, and were staying in naval quarters, before buying their own house, they had got themselves a dog, a little cocker spaniel puppy, and Carl had given it the name of Boris. Looking back, it was of course typical of his sense of humour, his way of laughing at the people around him, those he was fooling. Could it, though, also have been that a small, a minute, part of him unconsciously had wanted out, had wanted to get caught? With his clothes, too, the long coats with fur collars he sported later on, his 'spy outfits' as the children used to call them, had he been trying to announce something? Make a statement? Presumably once on the KGB payroll, however tired or disillusioned you may become, there could be no changing your mind. No 'I would like to tender my resignation, and thanks for everything'. Nothing like that; the only way out, death or to be caught – unless you considered the emergency defections to Moscow, notorious for ending in alcoholism, another form of death.

But then, with time passing, and after plying his trade undetected for over twenty years, perhaps he had felt so confident, so sure of his position, inviolable, that he no longer questioned his security (a job like any other, he had described it to Lilian); no longer questioned whether he might be rumbled one day. And in all probability he never would have been, had the matter rested solely upon his own competence. However, when treachery is your business, to be betrayed by a fellow traitor (in this case a KGB defector) would seem a fairly logical sequence of events, at any rate on the cards.

Headlines in national newspapers blazed sensational captions like: 'Biggest Spy since Philby!' There were diverse accounts of his capture, varying from his being snatched on a train in Eastern Europe, caught red-handed in Simonstown (but doing what exactly, nobody seemed to know) to – and this was eventually settled to be the correct version – an elaborate trap laid for him by the FBI in America. Scenes were painted of armed FBI agents bursting into his hotel suite and overpowering him while he sat drinking brandy with a man whom he believed to be simply a colleague on the same course that he was doing, but was in fact another FBI agent.

The extent of the damage he had done to NATO and the West was speculated upon, and any details they could rake up concerning his life in general, many of which, in the immediacy of their haste, they got wrong. In the

photographs he looked reasonably relaxed, and again
Lilian wondered if there wasn't some element of relief in
his expression.

When he had tried to recruit Lilian, he had told her that
he worked for the Russians, that he was a master spy, that
he ran a spy ring in Europe (for which she was required to
act as courier), that he was a double agent even, but he had
never mentioned being a betrayer of NATO secrets. This
now, in the newspapers that she read, seemed to be the
main object of concern. There appeared to be much
embarrassment over the question of his trial. He knew too
much, too many international secrets, to be allowed to
speak out in public. With his back to the wall and nothing
to lose, he might spill the beans about all sorts of highly
sensitive matters, including, it was hinted, controversial,
even clandestine, arms deals. It was decided the court
martial should take place behind closed doors, in camera.

Reporters came, hoping to talk to Lilian, to obtain or draw
from her the kind of personal reminiscences that might
interest the public, or throw light on Carl's character and
background – the usual sort of thing. They camped about
in hotels and, as she didn't answer the doorbell, hung
around in her road, questioning neighbours as to her
movements, with the idea of approaching her as she came
and went to work. So she absented herself, staying with
friends, leaving neighbours to explain to the reporters that
they were wasting their time, for even if they caught up
with her, she had no intention of uttering a single word;

they would get nowhere with her. And they – rather like Napoleon's army finding Moscow empty – running out of anything constructive to do, retreated back across the water whence they had come. Some left cards with telephone numbers – in case she changed her mind and decided to make herself some money – and all departed for good.

Her children were not quite so fortunate. One, at university in England at the time, preparing for exams, was harassed beyond endurance and finally exclaimed, 'I would be ashamed to force myself on another person's sufferings!' To which the reporter retorted, 'And I would be ashamed if my father was a spy!'

A friend said, later, 'Didn't you know the saying: "Never wrestle with a pig – you both get dirty, and the pig likes it."'

When the news had first broken of the dramatic capture and arrest of a high-ranking South African naval officer, whose years of training and some sea appointments had been with the British Royal Navy, on charges of spying for the KGB and passing on NATO documents, the main angle in the media had been the shock registered both in high places, and among friends and colleagues; and of course estimations of the extent of damage done by him over the long period that he had been successfully operating. Little by little, as one story broke after another of his alleged crimes and exploits, the mood turned from the initial reaction of excitement, almost fascination – a sensational new spy – to a feeling of punitive anger and revenge.

This Carl Hentze had been entrusted with a very senior position, and had betrayed the West for money and his own interests, duping his countrymen and allies; laughing at them, getting away with it for decades – he must pay the penalty. And the penalty for high treason was death. Now the speculation in the newspapers revolved around whether he would be hanged or shot by a firing squad.

For people who have had no personal brush with the death penalty, the question of capital punishment is an academic one: Is it wrong, morally, or justified? Should it be lawfully administered as a deterrent? Condoned as an unpleasant but necessary evil? For years Lilian had campaigned, as a member of Amnesty International, against all forms of capital punishment, writing letters to governments and heads of state around the world appealing for the release of political prisoners, clemency, demanding the abolition of the death penalty in all countries and in particular where people were still being hanged or shot in large numbers, or where they simply disappeared without trace. She believed that murder was murder, in whatever guise. She believed it wrong and barbaric, even more brutal when done in cold blood than something done in the heat and madness of passion – but she had never, for a moment, imagined just exactly how the family and relatives, people who cared about the condemned person, might feel.

Now she realised that for them it was possibly worse. For when you are dead, you are gone, but for those who are left, how is it for them for the rest of their lives? They would carry images of horror in their minds forever;

never, ever to be free of them. Just to imagine Carl standing while they put a noose around his neck, and then, with people watching indifferently, the moment of the drop, his head hanging sideways, his eyes . . . simply to think of it was enough to make her lose her reason. Or tying him to a post and blindfolding him, while a row of men lined up smartly and took aim . . . And if it was unbearable for her to contemplate, what would it be for the children? How would they feel? Their own father – good or bad, still their father. And on the appointed day, looking at their watches, thinking: 'In five minutes from now . . .'

She went to the Amnesty offices, and found Fergus, the director. 'How are you, Lilian? Are you all right?' he said warmly when he saw her. She had phoned in a message previously to say she wouldn't be in for a while, and he had assumed that she was sick. A couple of years ago she had reverted to using her maiden name, Prowse, around Dublin, and Fergus, recently replacing the last director, had never known her as anything else, so naturally he had no notion of a connection between her and the spy story going around.

'Can we talk without being disturbed?' she asked him.

'You don't look well,' he said, leading the way to the director's office. 'Should you be here?'

Walking past the room where she had worked on so many evenings, she felt herself strangely disconnected, a different person somehow; that had been then, and this was now – an enormous gulf between. She couldn't imagine being in there, laughing and chatting with the other voluntary workers.

'That South African spy all the papers are on about,' she said, as soon as they were sitting down, 'he was my husband once, and is the father of my children.'

'No!' he said, 'Really? I had no idea. Of course I knew you came here from South Africa, but . . .'

'There's a lot of talk he may be hanged.'

'Well, yes. Treason.'

'Can we send an official Amnesty communication to the South African government, saying we are following the case, and we are concerned that the death penalty should not be called for – just as we do for any other South African, black or white, anyone we fear they may pass a death sentence on?'

'We would have to get official permission,' he said.

'Of course. There's time. They said the trial will take months. Who do you have to get the permission from?'

'London,' he said. 'A special committee.'

'Thanks, Fergus. Will you ring me when you hear?'

'I will, of course,' he said. 'Take care. And Lilian . . .'

'Yes?' she said, from the door.

'I do understand how you must feel.'

She felt slightly better after that, and waited patiently. Then she got tired of waiting and went in again. 'Fergus,' she said, 'any news?'

Again they went to his office to be private. 'They said no,' he told her, hardly able to look at her.

[183]

'What do you mean, they said no?'

'I've been informed, by the top man himself, that Amnesty can't put on any pressure in this particular case,' he said. 'They don't want anything to do with it. It's too sensitive politically.'

'But Amnesty is not political!' she said, aghast. 'They campaign against all forms of capital punishment, regardless of the country or politics, and regardless of the crime! I know it, I've written hundreds of letters about it! Carl is just a person like anyone else, and the authorities are talking of hanging him! Fergus – he's the father of my children!'

'I know,' he said, looking miserable.

'But Amnesty opposes the death penalty!'

'I know.'

'But it's written: "All prisoners without reservation"!' Her voice sounded hysterical and she stopped, looking at Fergus's face for help.

'I'm sorry,' he said. 'Lilian, I'm really sorry.'

She left then. She couldn't face seeing anyone she knew in the lift, who might want to talk, so she went down the fire escape, the cement stairs at the back of the building. After one flight, she sat down and put her head on her knees.

Fergus, who had followed some way behind, uncertainly, came and sat with her until she was ready to continue on down. 'I'm so sorry,' he repeated several times, 'so very sorry.'

After that there was nothing more she could think of to do, so she blocked her mind and got on with her work and everyday life. She didn't avoid the newspapers, but neither did she go out of her way to read them. One morning, on the bus going to work, she saw looking up at her, from a paper on the lap of the man sitting beside her, the face of an old friend, a fellow-officer of Carl's, from the days of the Manadon Royal Naval Engineering College – and a caption: 'Hang him!' It was supposed to reflect the sentiments of their friend towards Carl. She felt almost physically sick, but could not remove her eyes from the familiar features. There had been a group of them, the whole class, all friends; they had danced at each other's weddings, attended christenings of first children, and then been dispersed all over the globe, to different ships, appointments, countries, as if to different worlds. Later, she bought a copy of the paper for herself and read of the shock the poor man had felt to discover his good friend had been a traitor amongst them all. He found it hard to believe, he told the reporter, almost impossible, but insisted that if Carl was proved guilty, he should be hanged.

Harsh words, but after her initial revulsion, Lilian realised he was just striking out blindly, without knowing the full implication of what he said; she began to think about how he might have felt – a kind of terror, for his own position; his career, the life he had built up for himself over so many years; all could be ruined by the past association, a firm friendship in good faith. Would he become suspect himself? Be put under surveillance? Would he miss out on promotions in the future, be passed over without explanation? Would his superiors just not *quite* trust him in the same way as they had before? But instead always be on their guard, on the watch-out, taking note of his every new acquaintance, where he went on holiday, even who his wife's friends were? And despite the violence of his outburst, she could understand, and she felt pity for him.

And how many others, she wondered, would be assailed by these same very legitimate fears, both in England and South Africa, feeling their lives compromised, tarnished, by their years of unsuspecting friendship or acquaintance with this Soviet spy? Even people who had the most tenuous connections with him would be affected, like the young RN officer she heard about, who got called in, somewhere in England, and questioned because his sister had been a class-mate of a Hentze child – simply been to the same school in Dublin, and sat in the same classroom. He's made lepers of us, as well as himself, she thought; it's not surprising that everyone is scrambling to disassociate themselves from him, they don't want to be lepers, too.

But there is always a reverse side to the coin; there were those people, she found, people on nodding acquaintance only, who were suddenly eager to talk to her. They would cross the road even, if she was on the other side, and say things like: 'You're Lilian Hentze, aren't you? Didn't you come here from South Africa, years back? That South African spy, Carl Hentze – well, my friend and I were wondering, was he your husband by any chance?'

And because news of that sort always goes around fast (and they, assuming that because she was divorced, she couldn't care less if he were hanged, drawn and quartered) people she barely knew would stop her in the street to ask, 'Will they hang him?' 'What do you think?' As if she was an expert on such matters. As if they weren't sticking knives into her.

The worst aspect for Lilian, the main issue she was conscious of, that she couldn't get out of her mind during those months of the trial, was how her children were feeling deep in those inner regions, where nobody really knows what goes on. Strong characters always, they appeared to be (indeed were) managing well, getting on with their lives, their friendships, their studies. But she feared for what they might have to cope with yet and she knew they feared for her too. Worrying about each other did not help. It was an added pressure which they could ill afford; better, they agreed, for each to do their own thing with their own friends, keep to normality at all costs, instead of getting into an unhealthy little huddle, the sort of soil in which terror thrives, while the waiting went on.

Thinking about this, Lilian turned her mind to a letter she had received a couple of months ago, from an old school friend. Jenny had been living in South America for many years and they wrote to each other, usually only once a year at Christmas to keep in touch. Without fail, each year Jenny would add a PS – 'Do come and stay!' But this particular year she had elaborated: 'Come on, Lilian, make the effort! Come for a visit! We love having friends out; we hardly ever see anyone – our nearest neighbours are more than a hundred miles away.' And she had added, knowing

Lilian's weakness; 'Horses – we've loads of them, you could ride all day!'

Jenny. It was her smile Lilian most remembered, and her hair so fair that it was almost white. And her honest, open expression. She couldn't hide anything or be devious to save her life. They had both been on the school tennis team, Jenny the captain, and Lilian in the third pair. There had been summer days, visiting other schools for matches, going flat out to trounce them, not always successful, but they weren't so tremendously competitive that it mattered one way or the other, just as long as it was fun.

She decided to sound out the situation at work, ask if it would be possible. Could they spare her? The response was immediate: Go! And not just for a week or two, a month or longer. They would find someone to fill her place temporarily. Money in advance would be made available.

'Jenny,' she wrote back, 'I'd love to come. What about now?'

I 2

It was cold and grey when she left, the sky thick as though it might start to snow at any moment. In the plane she took off her overcoat, folded it, and put it into an empty sports bag she had brought for the purpose. She would not be needing it for more than a month. Zipping up the bag she mentally added the entire story of Carl – from the beginning, up to the present revelations of the press; the speculations regarding the trial, and the dread of the sentencing – all of it, all, all, alongside the coat, not to be taken out, not even to be remembered, until the return flight. She had made up her mind that on no account would she talk about Carl's arrest to Jenny and Bill, and the chances were that they would not have heard about it, or if they had, would probably not have connected it with her, she had been divorced for so long now. She felt she needed, more than anything else in the world, not to have to think about it, to spend time in an environment where the issue simply did not exist. Just to be free of anxiety; to feel the sun heating her skin, the bright light of the south burning new sights and impressions into her.

She did not have long to wait; a stop-over in Miami, and Bill met her the next day in the teeming airport of Barranquilla. He himself had driven up from their area of Chiriguana, an eight-hour journey, so he had booked rooms in a hotel for that night, to be fresh for the driving the next day. Both needing to stretch their legs, they walked around the town that evening and had dinner in a noisy crowded restaurant. It had been a convenient trip, he said; he had been able to spend some of the day shopping for the house and the farm – they didn't get into town very often.

In the morning they loaded the Land Rover and early, before the heat, were already on their way, deep into the Colombian countryside. They talked, of course, and rem- inisced about people and places they knew, but all the while Lilian's eyes were as if she had no control over them, they seemed to be stretched wide open, marvelling at the mountains and ravines, the gigantic trees and dense undergrowth, the high waterfalls and deep rocky rivers, the dark eerie shadows and fiery sunlight. At intervals, when least expected, there would be a person, or persons, standing in the road, selling oysters in little cartons, with spicy sauces, and other delicacies, and they would pull in to the side and sample whatever was on offer – a far cry from McDonald's.

And Chiriguana was a far cry from Devonshire. But

after she and her friend had hugged and laughed and each exclaimed that the other still looked as they had at school, and they were sitting on the veranda of the long white-washed house, looking out over the mass of flowers and shrubs that was the garden – Lilian and Bill each with a glass of rum and pineapple – the differences didn't seem so great any more; life was life, wherever you were.

The ranch stretched further than the eye could see in every direction, even beyond the distant blue mountain range. Two rivers on their long journey to the sea cut through the dry savannah, flat grasslands with scattered bushes and trees, where cattle grazed peacefully. They had forty odd horses, some of which would be out to grass, some in foal, and the remainder kept in a corral to be used by themselves and the cowboys. Lilian could ride whichever one she liked, whenever she liked. Western saddles were used – always an ambition from her early days of Hopalong Cassidy films and Zane Grey books – and they were certainly as comfortable as she had imagined.

Looking at mountains and vast plains had always filled her with vague and unaccountable longings – for what, freedom? She didn't know, but somehow, with a horse you could point in any direction you liked, and simply become part of the landscape; it was as if she had found an answer to something.

Jenny, a potter, had built herself a kiln and, having her own things to do generally, understood and encouraged Lilian's contentment to do more or less nothing except ride long distances each day. Bill, however, had ideas of a more adventurous nature; she was to see something of the life and countryside further afield. She was to get the right idea of things, not just lounge in comfort and then go home. For example, the nearby village, five minutes away on horseback, was peaceful enough on weekdays but Saturdays she must see, for then the bandits would come down from the mountains for supplies, and they would sit around all day on wooden chairs and benches outside the shops and houses. If you passed that way on Saturdays, you didn't stop; you just kept jogging on through, not looking to left or right, or at least not appearing to. Lilian let her hair fall over her face so that she could look through it without noticeably staring at them.

They sat, hordes of them, drinking from bottles, chatting, shaded by the straw roofs of the houses, their sombreros on their knees, most with black moustaches; they dandled the small village children on their laps. Bill said that sometimes they kidnapped Europeans from their farms for ransom money. There was no point, he said, in hiding from them – they knew everything; who you were and where you were. If they wanted to kidnap you they would, and if they didn't, they wouldn't – it was quite simple. Some time ago they had kidnapped two neighbours from a ranch a couple of hundred miles away, a woman and her seventeen-year-old son, and kept them for six months while the ransom was got up. They hadn't been harmed, in fact they said afterwards they had been treated quite well, and given a copy of Marx to read to pass the time. Even though there were no real measures you could take to prevent this kidnapping, occasionally Bill, if he heard something suspicious around the farm buildings at night, would sleep in a hammock on the veranda, with his shotgun across his chest.

Some distance away there was a very large river, a far run tributary of the Amazon, and it was decided that Lilian should see something of the way the river people lived, in the villages along the banks. They drove to the river by Land Rover, and then switched into a waterbus, a long dug-out canoe with an outboard motor fixed to the back. It was already filled with men and women of all ages, and a lot of excitable children who kept trying to rock the canoe for kicks. Unhurriedly the bus pottered down the brown river – alligators visible under the muddied surface of the water, monkeys jumping in the trees – stopping at the various fishing villages along the banks on either side for passengers to get in and out. The villages, straggling groups of wooden huts with roofs made from straw or dried banana leaves, all looked much alike, but after about an hour, coming around a wide curve in the river, Bill indicated and said something, and the long canoe pulled in at the side of a muddy and slippery bank for them to get out.

Whether or not they were expected, Lilian could not quite make out, but they were given a friendly and noisy welcome and shown dinner (fish stew) cooking in a black pot over a fire. Bill and Jenny got into a long conversation with a man and his wife, whom it appeared they had not seen for some time, and there was clearly much news swapping. Lilian, unable to speak Spanish, went and sat among some children, who were not in the least put out or hampered by the language problem, but were instead highly diverted by the fact that her hair was fair (and Jenny's still fairer), a continuing source of amusement and giggles throughout the day.

There was a great deal of activity in the river. Some men had netted a sizeable shoal of silvery wriggling fish, and the women and their older daughters were sitting around in the village canoes cutting, cleaning, washing each fish, and packing them thickly with salt. This way they could be kept, taken down the river to towns and sold in large quantities. In the shallow water below the mud banks, large healthy-looking pigs waded knee-deep, snapping every so often into the water to catch their own supply of fish. One crafty sow had sneaked up to the side of a wooden canoe and, leaning in, was gobbling from the heap of fishes waiting to be cleaned. No one seemed to mind too much, the women just waved it away and shouted at it from time to time.

How do you gauge poverty? Lilian asked herself. Here, if you got ill, you probably died and that was it. No doctors, no clinics, no hospitals. And these children that she was sitting amongst, in their torn clothing and with bare feet, what education was there for them? What opportunities to make something better of their lives? And these fishermen and their wives, what rights had they got? What protection from dictators, and drug barons, and bandits? On the other hand, she thought, looking at the spontaneous water-melon smiles, trusting and friendly; the brown and healthy limbs; the buzz of lively conversation coming from the various groups, the men fishing, helping to clean the fish, the women cooking, the older men and women attending to the fires and minding grandchildren; all showing a keen interest in the daily events of their lives. On the other hand, she repeated to herself, take the poverty in Ireland, right there in the inner city where I work, except for the growing numbers of homeless, poverty generally means a corporation flat or house with bath and toilet, running hot and cold water, a cooker and most likely a fridge, certainly a television; and some kind of regular welfare allowance. It means schools for the children, and access to doctors, clinics, dentists, hospitals. But where in those grim and mean city backstreets, where poverty is, where boredom, despair and frustration are, where do you see such happy smiles, trusting and friendly? Where do you see all ages together taking a keen interest in the daily events of their lives?

The fish stew was served. It was superb. The plates were banana leaves.

'We will be moving the herd tomorrow. It will be a long ride, beyond the foothills of those mountains over there. Would you like to help?' Would she ever!

All day they pressed forward, keeping the cattle in a long continuously moving stream. The cowboys, whooping softly, cantering now and then to head off a recalcitrant steer, were fanned out behind the herd and around the sides. There was no sense of urgency, just vigilance. Incidents were few. After some time Lilian, comfortable in the western saddle and long stirrups, felt simply a part of the overall rhythm, the concerted almost fluid movement, the muffled sound of thousands of hooves on the go. Every so often one of the huge lumbering bulls would turn in protest and make threatening gestures at the nearest horse and rider; then, not bothering to carry it through, would rejoin the herd and continue on. 'They're just like us, really,' Bill remarked, passing on his favourite roan mare, 'they like to object now and then, but in the end it's too much trouble to keep it up.'

Jenny's daughter and son-in-law had arrived from England. He was a photographer and keen to get up high into the mountains. A horseback camping expedition was planned. They took a pack mule to carry the food and each person strapped his own hammock to his saddle. It was very simple – no tents, no sleeping bags.

'If you camp on the ground,' Sarah told Lilian and her husband, Mark, who also didn't know the practicalities of Colombian life, 'snakes and horrible insects come into your tent. There are sort of land crabs that come up through the earth and make holes in your groundsheet. So you tie your hammock in the trees and sleep well out of reach of them all.'

They had to go some way across the savannah first, ford a river at the shallowest point, and then, little by little, gentle slopes first, they started to ascend into the foothills. Beyond were the mountains, a lesser region of the great Andean range. After some time, the undergrowth between the trees thickened, and there was only a narrow path. They had to stop riding in twos and talking; it was only possible to go in single file and even then it was necessary sometimes to lean down low over the saddle to avoid being scraped off by hanging branches. It was very hot. And still. Sounds of animal life were all around. Colourful blossoms weighed down the branches of trees, and evil-looking orchids sprouted and cascaded from the most unlikely places. They went on, and up. The path, ridiculously narrow now, with loose stones and unsteady boulders, was running along the sheer side of a ravine. 'Don't look down,' Jenny called from behind. 'We'll be all right.'

'We will?' It didn't seem possible. But there was no going back, you could only go forwards. You'd go over the precipice if you tried to turn your horse.

They rode on all day, through gorges, crossing stony dried-up river beds, passing under enormous flowering trees, and at dusk made camp in a grassy clearing like a small field, beside a river. After a rest and a swim they got down to making a fire and cooking. It felt really good, sitting on the rocks half in the river, eating by firelight. The horses were let loose to forage for themselves.

'What if they wander off?'

'They won't. They'll still be there in the morning.'

She lay awake a long time in her hammock, looking up

at the stars in the silent universe. They were so bright and so near. In fact, after some time she felt closer to them than she did to the ground beneath her. It was as though she had lost touch with the ground and all that was connected with it – life on earth, as we say. She felt like Yeats's Chinamen: 'There, on the mountain and the sky, On all the tragic scene they stare.' She felt that from where she hung in her hammock among the stars, she was looking down on the whole scene of mankind; the wars, the exploitations, the cruelties, the betrayals, and that she was far, far away from it all; that it no longer touched her.

She had come into the house with Sarah, both laughing, exhilarated, adrenalin running high; having had a lucky escape. Returning across the savannah from a late afternoon ride, and on the point of putting the horses into a last gallop, Sarah had said, in a quiet voice, almost a whisper, 'Keep walking, and come this way with me.'

'Why, what's the matter?'

'Do you hear that noise, that sort of hum? It's killer bees. Don't talk, just follow.'

Lilian whispered back, 'Why don't we gallop? Get the hell out?' But she did as she was told, and they walked, veering to the left, in silence. And because they were listening intently, trying to gauge the distance and whereabouts of the swarm, it seemed that suddenly they heard everything around them, every minute sound; the dry grasses crackling under the horses' hooves, birds calling, the rustle of a snake or lizard, and all the time the menacing hum of the bees. Sometimes it seemed even louder, as if they were nearer, and Sarah, with a look, would indicate to change their direction. For some time they zigzagged across the savannah, as quietly as they could, sweating in the heat, almost holding in their breath for the moment they would no longer hear that angry throbbing sound.

Later, when they were well and truly out of range of the bees, Lilian asked, 'Do they really kill?'

And Sarah had said, 'They can. Or you might only lose a leg or an arm. A man from around here lost a leg two years ago. But never try to gallop away from them – they hear the noise and come after you. And make no mistake, they get you.'

'It must be strange,' Lilian said, 'living as you do, between England and Colombia – there, where people try to be insured against every possible contingency, and here, where hazards such as that you might be attacked by killer bees or bitten by snakes or kidnapped by bandits, are present around you all the time.'

'I was brought up this way', she said, 'I prefer it. Come on, we can gallop now.'

And so they had come in, hot and laughing, going straight to the kitchen for some iced juice.

Bill had returned from another shopping trip, and the kitchen was cluttered with boxes of groceries and such supplies as were unobtainable in the nearby village. Sarah took her drink and went for a shower. On the table a current *Time Magazine* lay flicked open. There was a photograph of Carl and Lilian caught sight of the words: 'High-living spy . . . extravagant tastes . . .'

Jenny was looking at her. 'You don't have to talk about it,' she said, 'but I thought you might want to.'

'It's taking so long,' Lilian said, sitting down, a sudden dreariness making her tired. 'The trial. It's in secret, in camera, behind closed doors, so nobody knows what's happening. But the newspapers go on and on, speculating about whether he might be hanged or put in front of a firing squad. I can't stand it. People seem to think that because I'm divorced I shouldn't care. Care? Of course I care! But more than anything I can't bear thinking how the children would feel if . . . Can you imagine? Their father?'

Jenny had been married before, and divorced. Sarah was from her first marriage. 'I would feel exactly the same as you,' she said. 'Exactly. And you are right to shut out the waiting; to keep strong. Nothing is worse than dreading something that might or might not happen. The uncertainty alone could destroy you. Are your children doing the same?'

'Yes,' Lilian said, 'with their friends. What else is there to do?'

They didn't speak of it again. Only the fact that now and again Jenny would shoot reassuring smiles to her, affirming her support and encouragement, was enough; for Lilian it was a new experience to share her feelings with another, to feel that person understood.

Sadly, Lilian was only to learn much later that already then, Jenny had known herself to have cancer. She must have felt Lilian had enough to be sad about, for she said nothing at the time they were together. On the other hand, perhaps she simply did not feel ready to talk about it.

The ordeal of returning to an outcome uncertain, unforeseeable and unpredictable was tempered by the desire to see her children, and by the knowledge that whatever was to happen, the eventuality had to be faced and got through. Tomorrow has to come, and then the next tomorrow; life could not be dammed up like a stream, or put off. As the plane made its way towards the wintry north, Lilian's mind turned to the zipper bag in the overhead locker containing her overcoat and she remembered how, coming, she had, figuratively speaking, packed Carl and everything connected with him alongside her coat and mentally labelled the bag 'Not required until return journey'. That he had done a Houdini and she had been obliged to see his face smiling cheerfully, brazenly even, from the inner pages of *Time Magazine* on Jenny's kitchen table, was typical of him. It was his style, and she wondered if there was, if there might be, a chance he would yet find his way out. Nothing would surprise her. She dozed, imagining different scenarios: a KGB rescue operation, armed men bursting in on the trial, in the same way that the FBI were said to have burst in on him in America, or him turning up in Ireland in his long coat with the fur collar, and a newly made plastic face, trying to convince her and the children who he was, but finding that with the new face he had been given a new voice, that could only speak in Russian, so they were not able to understand what he was saying . . .

When she woke they were already over Ireland, and a few minutes later the plane started to make a wide descending circle around Dublin; they were over the bay, and she could see the mountains beyond Dun Laoghaire. She got down her bag and took out her coat.

13

She had been back some time before she became aware that there was always a face at the window of the apartment directly above her own. A new occupant had moved in while she was in Colombia. The face was there whenever she came in, and whenever she went out, as if on the lookout for her. In fact somebody else, a friend or one of her children, had noticed it first and, the face being that of a man, soon everyone was joking about it: He must fancy you!

Then he began to be everywhere around the building as well; in the hall, in the garden, up in the laundry room at the top of the house where residents used the washing machines. He started saying, 'Hi!' when she passed him, and trying to get into conversation with her, but he had a South African accent which put him out of luck, for it didn't incline her towards being friendly, the reverse in fact. Too many memories. He seemed to be an athletic type with close cropped faded blond hair and a hard expression. Despite that he was obviously attempting to make himself pleasant.

Because she always kept on walking when he addressed her, in passing on the stairs or in the hall, he made a point of cornering her in the laundry room when she would be in the middle of loading or unloading a machine. One time he told her that he had got a couple of bottles of wine in his flat, would she like to drop in later for a glass or two? She wouldn't.

Evidently feeling he was not getting anywhere, he tried a different tack, again in the laundry room. This time he produced a photograph of himself and Carl together, in diving gear, and told her they had been friends. He held out the picture to her and said, 'My name is Clive. I'm a friend of your husband's, an old friend from way back.'

She glanced at it. It was Carl all right. It had obviously been taken a long time ago; Carl looked very young in it, vulnerable somehow; he was laughing, enjoying himself.

She said coldly to the man who called himself Clive, 'He's not my husband now. And if you were a friend of his, how come I never met you? How come he never invited you to our house?'

'Ach, I was away, doing other things, in other parts of the world. You know how it is.'

'It's a small navy,' she said. 'You get to know everyone in it. Strange I never met you, or even heard of you.'

'We were good friends,' he insisted.

'If you say so,' she said. 'Well, I must get on.' And having finished loading and setting the machine, she went down the stairs, leaving him alone with his picture and his foiled intentions, whatever they were. What did he want? Was he a spy too? The photograph had upset her, seeing Carl as he had been; young and full of fun.

Passing the door of Clive's flat, the one above her own, she paused and looked at it curiously. All the doors in the house were large, solid and painted with a heavy white gloss paint. They were identical, except . . . and now she looked at his door in surprise. How was it possible that having passed this way so often on her way to and from the laundry room she had never before observed that this particular door, this only, had been fitted with an outsize and very complicated looking new brass lock – round, like a safe lock, with a sort of dial? Why just Clive's door? He must have put it in himself. It was a monstrous affair – had he got permission from the landlord? What had he got in there, for God's sake? Who did he think was going to break in? And why draw attention to himself, make people suspicious? And then she thought of how many times she herself must have passed this door and not noticed the excrescence on it. And who of the other tenants, even if they did notice it, would give it more than a passing thought? They would just think him a bit of a nutter, bit of an eccentric – plenty of those around.

It preyed on her mind. What the hell was this man up to? Whatever it was, it was definitely connected with her. The fact of his having that photograph of himself and Carl together was no a coincidence, like he just happened to have brought it with him on holiday. So why was he here? In the flat above her own? If he had come to exterminate her, he would hardly have taken up residence. Or would he? And why would anyone want her exterminated? Now that Carl had been caught, she could no longer be considered a threat. The beans had been spilled after all, by somebody else – the KGB defector by all accounts – so by rights she should at last be off the hook, free of everything connected with Carl's world, that whole sub-culture of treachery and crime. So why this now? Why had this unpleasant-looking character turned up to plague her? He gave her the eerie feeling that for him, either to get a woman into his bed, or to arrange her demise, would be one and the same, immaterial, of equal consequence to him, and she avoided him at all times, always looking before venturing into the hall, or entering the laundry room.

Meanwhile, having realised he was not going to gain Lilian's friendship or confidence, and probably bored by his lack of success and by the fact that she was out at work all day, so he couldn't even annoy her, Clive's main energies now seemed directed towards the feud he was having with the tenant of the hall floor flat. This was a woman (a single parent of mature age, with a son) who dressed expensively, in good taste, and tried to give the impression of being well-off, while at the same time ignoring and looking superior to the rumours that went round of her being in dire straits and behind with her rent.

Presumably to save money, she had run leads from all

her household appliances, including her television, under her door and across the hall to the electric sockets on the other side. Combined with this outrage (as Clive considered it) was the fact that the impressive entrance, the rather grand hall of the old house, was constantly filled with steam from long-forgotten kettles, left out to boil at all times of night and day, not to mention the danger of tripping over or electrocuting oneself from the array of damp wires and leads which ran like veins across the carpet. It seemed to be driving Clive mad with rage; he was invariably in the hall, half enveloped by steam, haranguing the other tenants, trying to get up a posse against the woman. Unfortunately for him – and difficult for him to understand, knowing nothing of Ireland – the general attitude of 'Sure, if she's hard up for money, poor thing . . . and mind you, there's the boy to think of – what's the harm in it after all?' (probably delivered more to deflate his self-righteousness than in actual pity for the woman) only further infuriated him. Disgusted, he bought himself what looked an inordinately expensive water speed contraption on a trailer, and from then on regularly took himself off to fly around Dublin Bay in a wet suit, to pass the time of day.

She grew resigned to his presence around the place, the way one grows resigned to toothache or other infirmities, that is to say she saw him as something unpleasant that one could do nothing about. When their paths crossed she nodded or said good morning in tones of minimal politeness, and he replied in kind, having given up saying 'Hi!'

and attempting to be chatty. He still watched her from his window quite blatantly; he knew she was aware of it, and she made sure that he knew she was; that she was keeping a weather eye on him. Was he trying to intimidate her with his sinister presence? If he was, he was out of luck, for as she settled back into her work, her mind taken up by the various crises surrounding the children and families she was involved with, she felt she no longer had the energy for extra problems. Coming home tired at the end of the day, she rarely bothered now, even to look up and see if he was standing at the window.

One evening she came in as usual and shut the door behind her. Goodness, she thought, feeling ashamed, did I really go out and leave the place in this mess? That's not like me. And what was I doing with my files out of the cupboard like that, my papers all over the floor?

As she tried to remember, the voice of reason came to her, cold and clear: You were not doing anything with your files – and you didn't leave the place in this mess.

No, I didn't, I definitely did not! What then? She went over and started picking up her papers from the floor, looking at them, and re-arranging them back into the appropriate files. It seemed to her in those moments that history was repeating itself. She had been burgled once before, years ago when the children were still small; some family silver had been taken. Nearly all the apartments in the square had been done at that time and somehow the knowledge that a thief had been doing the rounds and she had simply been included, had lessened the impact; it hadn't upset her, she hadn't felt personally targeted. This now, was it different? Why on earth would anyone want to look at her papers? What were they but her children's old school reports, pictures and letters; bits and pieces of family interest only; and in separate files, copies of reports she had written concerning her work. Who in the world would break in to look at these?

Had someone broken in? They must have done. How else could they have got in? Not through the windows, they were too high from the ground. She went to inspect her door. There was no sign at all of forced entry, everything was as normal, no new marks. She felt slightly nauseous and very angry, and was just wondering what to do – would she ring a friend? – when she became aware that some drawers were slightly ajar – her desk drawers. She pulled them out further, a feeling of panic in her now. The person, whoever it was, had been everywhere; nothing had escaped his filthy hands. The drawers had all been rifled through, everything was in a mess, chaotic.

There was a small box, containing what had been her grandmother's ring, her English grandmother. Ah, that was what it was all about then, was it? An ordinary burglary like before? It was gold with a large diamond in it – not her style, but she kept it for sentimental reasons, a link with the grandmother she had never known, who had died when Lilian's father was still a boy. She opened the box, knowing what she would see and sure enough the ring was gone.

'Why are there such bastards in this world?' She sat down, miserably, not even inclined to phone anyone now.

Of course it wasn't *that* bad. It wasn't a tragedy after all, no one had been hurt. Even her grandmother's ring was only a ring. It wasn't anywhere near as bad as the situations she came across at work every day – real tragedies of poverty, drunkenness and violence, children's whole worlds falling apart, shattered – it couldn't be compared. But nevertheless, she was only human, and the fact was she felt vandalised, her privacy had been vandalised, and it sickened her.

Then she noticed her address book, lying open, face down on the floor behind her desk. There was something odd about it. She went over and picked it up. It was thinner than it had been. Looking through she saw that a good few pages had been removed, but carefully. And suddenly she knew, for certain, without the slightest doubt – it was Clive, probably looking in her address book for family friends who might be contacts of Carl's.

Her first instinct was to fly up the stairs, bang on his door and confront him. But then she imagined him feigning innocence; slightly offended – how could she think such a thing of him? Offering his assistance, being the gentleman, was there something he could do to help? And she became even more inflamed. Of course he wasn't going to admit it. So what could she do? She felt a great need to do something, not just let him away with it, but what?

She told all her friends about the break-in, everybody. After long years of having to be secretive, having to keep everything inside herself, it was a relief to complain and

give vent to her outrage, and to feel a response of sympathy.

One friend knew people who knew people, as they say
in Ireland. 'Wait,' she said, when Lilian told her she was
going to make a complaint at the local garda station. 'It's
not the gardai, the ordinary police, you need. It's security.'

'How do I go about that?'

'If you like, only if you like, I can mention it to somebody who will mention it to somebody else. He'll be sym-
pathetic, I know. He'll do something about it.'

'OK,' said Lilian. 'Thanks. I would like it. I'd be glad to
feel there was someone on my side.'

So a man from the Special Branch was sent round; a tall,
broad-shouldered Kerry garda, with dark curly hair and
good teeth; a nice man. 'Well,' he said, after presenting
himself, 'you are Lilian Hentze, then?'

'Yes,' she answered, 'I am.'

There was a silence before he prompted, '. . . and you
have a problem?' He was smiling at her, looking amused,
she thought.

'I certainly do!'

'Right then,' he said. 'Tell me about it. You don't mind if
I sit down?' And he settled himself comfortably, still
smiling.

She thought how best to condense her story. 'You do
know that I was once married to Carl Hentze, the South
African who has been arrested for spying?'

He inclined his head. 'I do indeed.'

'Well,' she said, 'I've lived peacefully in Ireland for years, bringing up my children, getting on with my own life and now I'm being hassled by another South African. Maybe he is a spy too. He has moved into the apartment above mine, he watches me, he follows me around and tries to get into conversation with me, and last week he broke into my flat here and ransacked it.' She was almost trembling with indignation, but when she looked at the garda, she could only see amusement, and a sort of admiration on his face.

'Sure, Lilian,' he said, 'I'd say you're well able for him. It's a fine woman you are.'

'What!' She could hardly believe it. 'What do you mean I'm well able? I'm not at all! I tell you, my place was ransacked! I came in from work and found all my files out, papers all over the floor – they'd been gone through, my drawers had been gone through too – and my address book, can you believe it, pages had been taken out!'

Looking more serious, the Special Branch man said, 'Was anything missing? Stolen?'

'Yes,' she said, 'my grandmother's ring.'

'Ah then,' his face seemed to clear, 'it might have been an ordinary burglary, mightn't it? There are plenty of those around this area – you know, big houses. Sure, you can't be certain it's the man upstairs.'

'Of course it's the man upstairs! Why would an ordinary burglar go through my papers, my files? Why would he take pages from my address book?'

'He might,' the garda insisted, 'you never know with people, Lilian, you can get some odd ones, believe me.'

Lilian felt she was getting nowhere. She didn't want

sympathy so much as action. 'Look,' she said, 'why don't you take some fingerprints? Then you can go up and get prints off his door, too. I'll show you which it is.'

He was laughing at her and shaking his head. 'Are you telling me to go and take fingerprints?' He seemed to think it very funny. 'Seriously now, I don't think you need worry any more. It was probably just an ordinary robbery. Go down to the station and give them a description of the ring. They might even get it back for you, they catch the thieves sometimes, you know.'

'And the man upstairs . . .?'

'Just because he's a South African doesn't mean he had anything to do with your little break-in, does it now?'

'This South African,' she said, 'has been hassling me for months. He even tried to show me a photograph of himself and my ex-husband together, to prove they are friends. Frankly, I couldn't care less if they are or are not, except it probably means he's a spy too. Me, I want to be left in peace. I want protection from this man.'

The big garda sighed as if faced with a difficult problem, and looked at her sorrowfully, so she added, 'I know the Universal Declaration of Human Rights practically by heart. I worked for Amnesty for years. Article Twelve says: No one shall be subjected to arbitrary interference with his privacy, family, home or correspondence, nor to attacks upon his honour or reputation. Everyone has the right to the protection of the law against such interference or attacks.'

When she finished he gave a burst of laughter and said,

'By God, Lilian, I was right! You *are* well able. I should think you'd be well able for anyone!'

'No,' she said, 'you've got it wrong; I'm not remotely well able, really I'm not – that's why I'm asking for protection!'

After he had gone she felt lonely, let down, exposed to all manner of unknown dangers. She had no one to help her, and this enemy, this unsavoury character could just come in and out of her flat whenever he chose, leaving no trace, no sign of forced entry on the door, and for her there was still no security, no redress, no protection.

When she next saw the friend and described to her the disappointment she had felt concerning the visit from Special Branch, the friend's expression became furtive, almost guilty, as if she had information she did not wish to impart. 'Lilian,' she said, and then stopped, hesitating.

'What is it?' Lilian asked. 'You're hiding something.'

'Lilian,' the unfortunate woman tried again, 'you won't like this . . .'

'Never mind, go on.'

'Well, I've heard more about your case now, things I didn't know before. And, well actually, it seems that this South African man is just doing his job – and the authorities don't want to hamper him, get in his way. They can't go taking his fingerprints, and arresting him for breaking in.'

'His job! What job? Being a spy?'

'No, that's the point – he's probably been sent to investigate *you*, to find out if *you* are a spy.'

[214]

'To investigate *me*? To find out if *I'm* a spy!'

'Don't get angry. People have to do their work, you know, and you are bound to be considered suspect, after all, when you think about it. Apparently you've been under surveillance by Irish security for ages – they believe you are 'clean', but the South Africans also need to satisfy themselves – it's understandable.'

'I don't know if I can take all this,' Lilian said. 'It's too much for me.'

'If you've nothing to hide, you might as well take no notice, and let this man, this BOSS man (he would be from BOSS, I suppose?), let him just get on with it. He'll go away when he is satisfied.'

'What do you mean, *if* I've nothing to hide?'

'Oh, sorry!' and the woman laughed affectionately. 'Come on, Lilian, don't be touchy!' And then she looked again and said in a different tone, 'Oh come on, Lilian, don't cry!'

'So Clive's the "good guy" and you're the "bad guy"!' Her friends at work were determined to joke her out of her depression.

'He's not a "good guy", not by a long shot – you only have to see him! And these people have the nerve to call their work "intelligence"! I've never seen anyone less intelligent-looking in my life!'

But they were not prepared to listen to her. Lilian, they insisted, had got it all wrong. Poor Clive had been sent to Ireland to unmask Lilian the super-spy!

'He's scared as hell, thinks she's going to knife him in the back if he takes his eyes off her!'

'That's why he put the special lock in his door – to keep her out!'

'And that's why he broke in and looked in her cupboards – to see what sort of weapons she might attack him with!'

'No, no – he didn't break in, not through the door. He came down to her window on a rope!'

'Yes – in his wet suit, with a box of chocolates . . . Milk Tray of course!'

'He probably has fantasies about her – that she keeps a revolver in her stocking . . .!'

There was nothing for it, she could not do other than laugh with them as, wiping their eyes, they regaled themselves and each other with her imaginary exploits. There was a funny side, she had to admit.

But inside she felt wounded by the situation in a way that her friends wouldn't understand; that almost certainly no one who had not been a refugee of some sort would or could understand. She had come, with her children to Ireland many years ago now; reared her children here, come to love both the country and the people. That anyone might think, even for a moment, that she would abuse that welcome, betray it, came as a shock to her; just as from the personal point of view it shocked her to think she might be suspected of duplicity, a devious underhand nature. And it was mortifying, to say the least, to know she had been under surveillance by the Irish security – like a criminal; mortifying to have her honour held in question, to have people discussing whether she might have been leading a life of lies all this time. She resented the imputation Carl had brought upon her, here where she had made her home.

A man she had known a long time (who liked reading books about people like Philby, Maclean and Burgess) had admitted quite openly to her that he and his wife had discussed the possibility that she might be a 'sleeper', planted years ago, to be re-activated if and when required. They didn't think she was, he told her. They had come to the conclusion that it was unlikely, but added that they could never be sure, could they? And who knows, Lilian thought, how many others are saying the same?

Fruitless to ask herself questions like what made Carl think he had the right to inflict all this on her and the children; fruitless because the sort of person who takes up espionage is hardly likely to care about moral issues such as the effects his treachery might have on others. The only remaining question then was why? Why had he wanted to do it?

14

Generally speaking, Lilian had always believed in every person's right to privacy concerning their actions and decisions in life; their right to make mistakes and find their way, pursue their star, without other people interposing themselves – and she felt the best, without doubt, was for each to concentrate on his own affairs and leave others to do the same.

However, in the case of Carl, whose decision to work for the KGB had so affected her entire adult life – and the lives of so many others besides – she felt not only the need and the right, but the obligation, too, to look at his decision and try to understand, or at least think about, why he had made it; what influences or impulses had urged or coerced him into switching from his chosen career (and right at the beginning of it) to take up a clandestine life of espionage; to be a spy, whose basic role was to betray trust.

'Tell me what you want,' says a Chekhov character, 'and

I will tell you what you are.' What had Carl wanted? An attractive and popular young man at the time, liked and well-thought of by practically everyone, free, not yet married; had he simply fallen prey to the temptation of money? Excitement? Adventure? The attraction of power? Had he been flattered at being singled out for recruitment? Was there a feeling of self-importance? Did he feel superior, knowing things that others didn't?

Of course, there aren't always explanations for what people do. Perhaps he did it only because he could, he had the opportunity, like people who climb Mount Everest because it is there. It's easy enough to ask why did he not stop to think? But would there have been any adventures – any of the dramas and tragedies we love to read or see enacted – if people had stopped to think? What, for example, if Othello had stopped to think? Or if Macbeth had been able to think clearly instead of being blinded by ambition? Would there have been wars or revolutions? Would people fall in love? Not stopping to think – hasn't it always been the human condition?

Then what about the saying 'Character is destiny'? Asked about characteristics valuable for spies, a certain MI6 chief listed: being ruthless, without scruples, and unbothered by conscience; not being subject to panic when frightened; when in danger being stimulated to clearer thinking and to better decision-making, and being prepared to obey orders. From her knowledge of him, she would agree that Carl probably had all those qualifications. Added to that, he was not only a convincing liar, a con-

summate liar, but he actually enjoyed lying. It appealed to his sense of humour. She could remember him talking about fishing one time to their host at a dinner party, and hearing the host, who actually had silver cups around the room for fishing, exclaim to him, 'Oh, I can see I'm talking to an expert!'

Afterwards she had said, 'But you've never fished in your life, have you?'

'No,' he had replied, obviously thinking it inconsequential.

'How do you know so much about it?'

'I read magazines. About everything. I like to be well-informed.'

'But you don't have to lie about it, do you, and pretend you fish yourself?'

'Why not, if I enjoy it?'

He had often told her he liked to keep people confused about him, and he certainly succeeded in that. She sometimes thought that if he were subjected to a lie detector, the machine would register stress levels if he told the truth.

There is, of course, the question of ideology. Clearly there are two main types of spy. The first is committed to some ideology or another – Communism or whatever else – and he is obliged then to relinquish all previously held values, all learned or innate patterns of behaviour; to jettison honesty and rectitude, frankness and integrity, for the sake of his cause.

The natural born spy has no such problems, for he probably has no ideology, and has not the above standards in the first place; if he appears to have them, they are merely part of his act. And she remembered, too, how when she had first known Carl, he had given the impression of being a dedicated Catholic, never missing mass on a Sunday, but (according to what he told her years later) in fact already working for, in the pay of, the Russian Communists. A protean man if ever there was one, he could be one thing one day, and another the next; using whatever was convenient at the time; expediency his key, his tool, his weapon – and his prop too; for to act, the actor need props, constantly.

She wondered then, had he taken up spying to escape from his real self, by acting a role? Actors, professional actors, have sometimes given this as a reason for having gone on the stage, and it has been said that spies also can be motivated by this same need; that they are people driven by dissatisfaction with themselves and a desire to become someone else, more exciting perhaps. And as an acting ability often goes together with an ability to deceive oneself, the spy who chooses a secret life – to become a character not his own – can avoid ever coming face to face with who he really is.

Maybe that was the way of it for some, she thought, but somehow she didn't see Carl there. Rather she found herself wondering if the truth might not, in his case, be the reverse side of that theory. Was it possibly a case like that of the 'tried and trusty', the 'indispensable' Nostromo who, although initially dependent on how he appears to others, eventually chooses to be his real self, to follow his true nature? The 'excellent' Capatez de Cargardores steals the silver and leads a secret life. Perhaps Carl likewise, in choosing espionage, was following his true nature?

This thought brought to her mind his descriptions of his earliest days. Very young when the Second World War broke out, he had seen his father led away from the house by policemen, and had later learned that this was because the Hentzes were German. South Africa, being under British rule, officially British territory, Germans were enemy and suspect. His father, an architect who had been practising some years there, was now interned on the grounds that he might (and according to Carl – but only later in his trial – did) have Nazi sympathies. At school Carl was jeered by other children, who hurled words like 'Jerry' and 'Nazi' at him, probably without even knowing what they meant. He would be sent home almost daily for fighting – the only way the child knew to salvage his honour. By the time Lilian met him he had perfected the art – or science – of making himself acceptable *par excellence*.

When they became engaged, many of his friends, and senior officers, too, approached her in private to assure her she was marrying 'the straightest man there is', and other such strong recommendations. One admiral (rather fatuously, she thought, but well meaning) said in her ear, 'You've picked a winner! We've been watching him since he was a cadet – he'll go right to the top!' Later, when they

were living in the Cape, and Carl was chief engineer on one
of the ships, the men who worked under him would take
Lilian aside at social functions and, rather movingly, tell
her of their admiration for him – even gratitude sometimes, concerning occasions where he had helped them to
sort out private family difficulties – instances she would
never knock, for they were quite likely just as much him,
as any of his other dealings.

She herself, twenty at the time, had been amazed when
on early acquaintance it transpired that they had almost
identical tastes; they liked the same books, the same music,
they had the same interests, held to the same values and
aspired to the same dreams. Too artless to see anything
suspicious in this (and as the generally held view is that we
are what our values are) she felt that even in so short a time
she had come to know him extraordinarily well. It never
occurred to her that he would simply be to people what he
saw they desired him to be.

It was a hard lesson he had learned as a child, that to be
acceptable, you had to be what 'they' wanted. But now he
had become an expert, and with his innate sense of
humour, a lightning wittiness, he had the ability to become
quite exceptionally popular wherever he went.

Why then, one might ask, with this acceptance, this
popularity, this unquestionable success, both in his career
and socially, was he not content to take advantage of it all
and enjoy it? Why jeopardise what he had? Was it that
through spying, his existence became more real, more
significant, took on more substance, than in the pretence

[223]

of being this paragon – which he knew he was not? Was it that he needed to escape from this pretence and fulfil his nature; needed to have the opportunity to be his intrinsic self?

In retrospect, it was easy to see how he must have chafed at the harness, requiring somehow to be fooling people, the stimulation of a contest. He seemed to find that when, for his own amusement, he would start lying or making outrageous assertions, the conversation would take on an extra dimension, have a tension to it. Then the more taut, the more alive he would become and the more he would enjoy it, seeing himself getting away with what-ever it was, not getting caught out. He liked to shock, to tell tall stories or make remarks that people did not quite know how to take. He would express views that were generally considered unacceptable and his friends, after a moment of uncertainty, would laugh and say, 'It's a good thing we know you, Hentze, or we might believe you mean what you are saying.' He would join in the laughter, often throwing Lilian a look which said, 'But I do!'

Yes, she thought, he was fun, he was likeable, there was no question about it. It's only when you got a glimpse of him laughing at the people he had duped, made fools of, that you had second thoughts.

But still the question, why had he become a spy? A lot is talked about the inflated ego of spies, their arrogance and almost insane vanity (Maclean is known to have consid-ered himself a 'diplomat and a statesman'). But wasn't this over-estimation of personal qualities more likely to be a result of spying, something that grew with time, rather than an original characteristic that might induce a person to spy? Lilian saw no clue there, but she did wonder at the same time just exactly how spies in general, and Carl in particular, saw themselves and their inconsistencies; the way that while in the process of spying, morality seems not to be an issue, but when caught there are flurries of ration-alisation. Suddenly, in self-justification, they all claim to be 'humanists' – although where their caring about human beings comes in is rather hard to see; treachery and betrayal implying the absence of, or disregard for, rather than the upholding of human values. And she thought again of Robert McDaid, murdered, given a fake suicide – and how many others besides? Humanists?

And she recalled all the years of her own life, while her children were small, of not knowing whether she might be meted out the same fate as McDaid, or have some accident or other forced on her. What sort of monsters were these spies that could treat people as expendable?

Which led to two further questions: firstly, could this abnormality be innate, a defect, a flaw already there in the embryo, that would steer an individual towards the under-world of betrayals and crime, or would someone like Carl, recruited so young, initially not have given a thought to the inevitabilities?

And secondly, should she take into consideration that his childhood had been dire? Not to say that everyone with a violent father is going to become a spy, but there is nevertheless evidence, and she had seen it through her work in Dublin, that continuous family violence does undoubtedly tend to erode respect and without that one thing, a person is left somehow baseless. In the end, she thought, isn't it respect for oneself, for others, for life and everything living, that is the single most important provision for keeping the feet on the ground and the eyes turned upwards?

She had liked her mother-in-law, admired her, too; a courageous woman, her life had been her three sons. That she seemed a trifle overly ambitious for them was after all a matter of opinion, and certainly not a crime. Her big mistake, in Lilian's view, was that she had put up with abuse and violence from her husband too long, staying in her marriage because, as she told Lilian, she could not bear the stigma of divorce, and the boys had thus paid the price. Eventually she did divorce; the situation, according to her, having become potentially dangerous; but by then the damage to impressionable eyes had been done.

For the young Carl, intensely unhappy, there had been incidents such as running away, clinging to the outside of a train; there had been rebellion, arguments, rows, threats and haranguings until, at the age of sixteen, he had made his way down to the Cape and joined the navy. From old photographs, you only saw the smile.

A man, reviewing his own experience, will look at the kind of things he chooses or rejects, and in doing so learn something about himself. But Carl's choices and rejections, she wondered, had they been red herrings, regarding the real person? In trying to understand the inner workings of this man – this spy, father, husband, betrayer, boy and fellow human being – it was as if a curtain had risen and hung in abeyance, just long enough for her to glimpse the whole immense universe of moral suffering. What she saw in that drawn-out moment had nothing to do with one mere individual; what she saw instead – even while an incorrigible mankind scrambled for worldly powers and successes – was a vast collective ache, a despairing search for the imperishable.

In trying to discover why Carl had chosen to lead the life of a KGB spy (the attempt had seemed like a long ride on a roller-coaster, the ups and downs, the circular rollings from anger to pity to incomprehension and back again) she had, of course, come no closer to a specific answer. In truth, she had not really expected to, it had not even been the point; for in life, she had learned, there are very few answers anyway. Rather the object had been to throw open the hitherto closed doors and windows of certain areas of her own life, let in some air and light, and she was glad now; she felt relieved, disencumbered somehow, liberated. To the question: why had he done it? All in all she felt the most probable reason was simply that it suited him and that it was more a case of human frailty than of vice.

15

Carl's trial, over some time now, was receding into the past. Sentenced to life imprisonment for high treason, he had begun serving his time in a prison in Pretoria and, although the prospect was grim, it was tempered by relief for those who has feared worse.

His second wife – the Swiss-German woman who had already been (according to Carl, years ago) functioning as a spy in the pay of the KGB before either knowing him or having anything to do with South Africa – had been sentenced to ten years.

Now that the strain of anxiety had been lifted; the unthinkable sentence of capital punishment removed from the offing, all who were concerned, and in particular the young people, the children, were free once more to get on with their own lives, saddened but no longer oppressed by dread.

The only person who could not get on with her life was

Mrs Hentze, Carl's mother who, Lilian heard with sorrow, had died from a stroke just days before the sentencing, the strain too much for her.

Lilian had seen photographs of her once, as a much younger woman, with her boys in the garden of their Pretoria home; the pictures redolent of hot still sunshine, the perfume of flowers, shady trees, the shouts and laughter of young children. Mrs Hentze had looked relaxed and happy, and Lilian, on hearing of her death, remembered the scene and was glad there had been anyway a modicum of happiness and joy in a life otherwise containing many disappointments. This last must have come at her like a thunderbolt from the unknown, and when she least expected it, for in her old age she was at last enjoying being able to sit back and see her ambitions realised – her three sons all successful, respected, professional men.

Recalling Mrs Hentze to mind, Lilian could almost hear her voice, her German accent, the way she rolled her r's – the very essence of her contained in the insistence, the conviction of her favourite self-admonishment: 'Try to think rightly!'

He would have known all along, of course he would, that he would not be hanged, or shot, or any other terminal measures be taken. It would have been out of the question; only small fry get made an example of, as a deterrent to other would-be traitors – he was much too big. To have him alive, incarcerated, was to have bargaining power in the international market of politics. Governments don't throw important pawns away, they push them around on negotiating tables, or put them on hold, to be brought out at the appropriate time. How could it not have occurred to her? Or anyone else? It was so obvious. And yet ordinary people like herself, who rely on what the newspapers choose to say, generally have no idea of the wheeling and dealing that goes on in secret. It was his world, not hers, and he would have known his own position perfectly well, which would have accounted for his relaxed appearance in photographs, despite the ghoulish speculations of the media. And the press, their interests lay in whipping up anticipation of revenge and punishment, to generate more world-wide interest in the case.

It was almost ironical to think that while others had been so burdened with dread, Carl himself would have been quite confident concerning the outcome of his trial, would not have lost a night's sleep over the future of his neck; perhaps even enjoyed the sensationalism. However, it is impossible to know the half of it; in all likelihood things must have looked bleak.

She hoped he would not be ill-treated. There was a long tradition of stories of prisoners in South African prisons being half-kicked to death and left to die on the stone floors of their cells. She didn't visualise other inmates bullying him (she remembered him warning her never to walk silently up behind him, that he was trained to kill in seconds) but there could be other cruelties, prison warders misusing their powers. However, Carl's flair for presenting the image people wanted was certain to stand him in good stead; he would probably have them eating out of his hand in no time.

She wrote to him. Her own life was going well at the time, but sometimes she thought of him, condemned to a prison cell for life, and she felt sorry for him. She believed in forgiveness and redemption, and she thought that life had perhaps given him a second chance; the opportunity to think, to contemplate, to review his life and change his mind. Maybe he could find a personal freedom, even there in his cell.

He wrote back, and after that a correspondence of sorts started up – censored and scrutinised by the authorities – difficult in that there was no common ground, no meeting of minds, but anyway, if nothing else, a form of communication.

From their polarised worlds (was Flaubert right – is there no such thing as reality, only perception?) they wrote only about small daily events. He told her he was growing tomatoes in the prison yard and studying for exams. It wasn't such a bad life, he said, easier than for millions who were struggling in the world merely to exist. He could order whatever books he liked, watch television, follow world affairs, take up courses on new subjects – and of course, take an interest in the progress of his lawyers – ever-active in pursuing every avenue that might lead to his release.

It didn't take long for her to realise there was no question of him re-thinking his life and ideas. As always, he seemed convinced that no possibility existed of his making mistakes; that whatever he did was right, and not because of any preconceived notions of right or wrong, but because it was he who did it.

Once, once only, he wrote that the thing he most regretted was the way he had treated her and the children. Was it true? Maybe he had moments of truth like anyone else? The trouble was, he could move you to compassion, but you never knew whether at the same time he wasn't laughing at you for being so stupid as to be taken in. How on earth were you ever to know? Maybe sometimes he really did think and care about such things, just fleetingly. Always her hope was that he would try to heal what he had done to the children, at least to try. Privately, her own thoughts were that he had spent his whole life in the dark, while imagining himself in the thick of things, and was clearly intent on staying there.

During these years, undreamed of changes were taking place in the outside world arena. In Russia, Communism had fizzled out, practically overnight, in favour of the free market. She wondered what he thought about that after all his years of working under Communist bosses, and she imagined him shrugging his shoulders and repeating, 'Oh well, it was just a job like any other.'

The next earthshaking events, inevitable but almost unimaginable at the same time, were happening in South

Africa itself; the release of Nelson Mandela, followed by
the abolition of apartheid and the approach of democ-
racy. Carl read the newspapers, watched the television and
continued to grow his tomatoes. Having found he had
backed the wrong horse, so to speak – Communism
having fallen at the fence, and clearly not intending to
resume the race – Carl, ever resourceful, scrutinised the
situation and decided that he was being held under the
incorrect category of 'traitor', that he was really a 'pris-
oner of conscience'; that he had all along been committed
to the ANC (African National Congress) and the abolition
of apartheid – which was why, he said, he had been spying
for the KGB for the last two decades. That he had mentioned no such leanings all the time she had known him,
not even when he had tried to recruit her years back, while
knowing her own abhorrence of apartheid, made her
think it more likely that he was simply finding himself
another mount, a new one, and getting back into the race.
It was a fact that ANC political prisoners were getting
released by the batch at that time, under the amnesty
between the government and the African National
Congress, and possibly he saw new and profitable horizons opening up for people who might be in the right
place at the right time.

In fact, when he was finally freed, some few years later,
following a request by President Boris Yeltsin, the request
was granted, according to the South African president
(F.W. de Klerk at the time), on the grounds of the 'new
situation in Russia, and the resultant improvement in

relations between Russia and South Africa'. Some two-way deal no doubt.

In the meantime, still in prison, but with the certitude now that things were moving in his favour – it being a period of great upheaval and possibilities – and that it would only be a matter of time before the prison gates would finally clang behind him, and he would be back in the world he was accustomed to, Carl sat his exams, achieving high marks, and kept up on world events in general.

The question of whether he might change during his time of imprisonment, alter his thinking, no longer crossed Lilian's mind. A world other than the one he knew and felt at ease in did not exist for Carl; he did not want another, he did not aspire to another. For him the 'real' world was the way he saw it; tough, you had to be smart to get on. And he was smart.

Years ago, one of his favourite anecdotes which, to his thinking, illustrated how children should be brought up if they were to get on in the world, seemed to her to encapsulate his whole general perception of the world he made around himself and lived in. The story (which it used to amuse him to relate to friends and then watch their reactions) was of a man who put his small son on a high wall and then coaxed him to jump to the safety of his arms: 'Come on, there's nothing to fear! I'm your Dad – trust me!' The little boy jumps and the father steps back, letting him crash to the ground. 'That will teach you,' the father says, '*never* to trust *anybody*!' And his friends would look shocked and then laugh, thinking he was joking.

So as he bided his time, his letters exuded a cheerful confidence that in time he would once again be in the thick of things – presumably this time in a legal capacity – where only the few, the elite, really know what's going on (the rest just think they do) and he would be in on the action. Being highly knowledgeable on military and security matters, he was well aware of his value. He could be extremely useful to future governments in an advisory role. Anything and everything was possible. It seemed he was completely unrepentant, utterly and totally oblivious of the fact that he was a convicted criminal, that he had spent twenty years disregarding the laws of every country he passed through, travelling under false passports, lying, selling secrets he had been entrusted with, deceiving governments and heads of state not to mention family, friends and colleagues; utterly and totally oblivious of having done anything wrong – other than get captured, and that had not been his fault. He had made no mistake, simply he had been betrayed.

And she, Lilian? Still, from time to time she felt the repercussions of that choice Carl had made a quarter of a century ago, and the life he had subsequently lived; still even though he had been caught and was serving his sentence, she knew that tabs were kept on her, whatever country she went to; the files on her were not closed. She imagined that any interest in her now was merely routine, but at the same time it was not pleasant to think it might last all her life – and the worst was not knowing what to expect.

One incident which brought her up sharply, reminding her that she was by no means free of 'them', whoever 'they' were, happened in Athens, where she was living at the time, writing, learning Greek and teaching English. She taught privately in people's homes, and had among her pupils, briefly, a military officer who needed, he said, to pass some army exams before being posted to Brussels. He spoke fast and fluently and could read well, but his grammar certainly left a lot to be desired, and so they commenced their lessons.

His house was high on a hill, overlooking the city, a hot climb to get to, but when she arrived they would sit in the large airy sitting room and his wife would bring them a tray with small Greek coffees, glasses of iced water, and sweet cakes she had made herself.

The situation was slightly strange, she thought, even from the beginning, because he, the colonel, didn't appear to be in the least interested in learning anything, and seemed positively to dislike being corrected. However, she put this down to the Greek male ego, and tried to persevere firmly and tactfully.

Then, one evening, at the close of the lesson, he left the room and returned with a document, several pages printed in English and clipped together. He put it into her hands and asked her if she would take it home with her and read it over the weekend. It would be a great help to him, he

told her, if she could then explain it at their next appoint-
ment – he had to be familiar with the contents for some
meeting. She looked at it, on the point of agreeing, and
saw on the front an official stamp which said, in capital
letters: NATO – TOP SECRET. She could not believe her
eyes. To start with, it didn't even look convincing, too
obvious somehow, childishly obvious. And if it was what
it purported to be, what on earth was he, a senior army
officer, who should know better, doing handing it out to
an English teacher he hardly knew? Urging her to take it
off the premises, remove it from his house? She wished
afterward that she had challenged him, asked him what the
hell he thought he was doing. Couldn't he understand the
words TOP SECRET? Was he a complete halfwit? But she
didn't have time to think. She casually handed it back to
him, without giving it a second glance, showing no interest, and said she was too busy. He should read it through
himself, she said, and write down any words he didn't
understand or couldn't find in the dictionary. It would be
good for him. It could be his homework.

It was only later, much later, that the full implication
revealed itself to her. My God, she thought, that could
have been the end of me. She could see the whole sce-
nario: a rapping on the door, herself opening it, police
bursting in (nobody does things calmly in Greece) and
seizing the document from her desk, shouting: 'NATO!
TOP SECRET!' at her, accusing her of stealing it from her
pupil, the army colonel, while he was out of the room.
And imagine, she said to herself, just imagine trying to

reason, trying to explain what really happened to a Greek police officer! Imagine trying to argue with any Greek official!

There would be newspaper stories of how she had posed as an English teacher to gain entrance to the homes of high-ranking military personnel, and then stolen top secret documents. Her connection with Carl would be gone into. There would be praise for the vigilant network of police intelligence, perhaps some individual promotions – a field day for all – and she would be left to rot in a Greek prison, with not one person in the world able to 'prove' her innocence.

There is a certain particular terror that comes from feeling helpless, and Lilian felt that terror now. It had been a trick. A trap had been laid for her, and she might so easily have fallen into it. It was as though violence was suddenly present in her life, evil; there were bad intentions directed towards her, and she knew not from where they came. And there was always the possibility of a next time – would other traps be laid for her that she might not spot, or be quick enough to avoid?

The end of this book is not going to be that by the time Carl is released, Lilian is sitting out lonely years, immured in a Greek prison, although it could have turned out that way. Rather it happens that she simply gets used to the intervention in her life of sometime consequences, sometime side-effects or spin-offs from Carl's choice of profession; gets used to the fact of his world, an entirely different value-based world, counterpointing her own. She finally accepts and gets used to these things, becomes accustomed, the way people learn to live with a disability or an abnormality.

Most people who know her are not even aware of her disability. You don't tell everyone you meet that you are prone to epileptic fits or that you are obliged to use a colostomy bag, if that is your case; you get on with what you are doing in your life and think as little about your disability as you can.

But at the same time, she no longer blocked her mind, as she had done in the past sometimes, to survive, to not be got down. Now she felt able to look at everything alike, seeing the unpleasant things as they were – as much a part of life as the good things; as merely fragments of what in many ways she had always felt to be a rather charmed and fortunate existence.

On the practical side, of course, it was still extremely annoying. In Dublin she had eventually moved flat to get away from the BOSS agent, Clive; at least not to have him overhead, with access to come in and out at will, almost certainly to have her rooms bugged. It had been expensive and inconvenient to move, not to mention that she had liked being where she was. Now she felt unsafe in Greece; it was not a place she would choose to find herself in trouble; not a place she would like to take her chances, as a foreigner, in a court of law.

On the other hand, the plus side, if she still stepped back from edges of pavements and railway platforms, it was more from old habit than any conscious thought. Hopefully, it was no longer necessary.

And concerning the future? She didn't think about it much. As always, it stretched out into the unknown like an infinite cloudless sky over a vast beach with as yet no footprints in the sand – calling always to men's hopes and aspirations and susceptibilities, making veiled and not entirely reliable promises of fulfilment beyond all expectation. She could afford to ignore it though – for the time being anyway, things were good enough as they were.